The Visionary Edge:

Leading Healthcare's Next Era Through Vision,
Innovation, and Strategy

Foreward By

Scott Becker

Founder of Becker's Healthcare

Author

Sumit Sharma MBA, FHFMA, SCPM, SSMBB

Executive Summary

The Visionary Edge: Leading Healthcare's Next Era Through Vision, Innovation, and Strategy is a strategic, story-driven playbook for healthcare leaders ready to shape—not just survive—the future of care delivery. Blending practical models, system-level thinking, and compassionate foresight, this book equips executives with the tools to lead through complexity and uncertainty.

Core Thesis

The healthcare system of the future won't be built by optimizing today's models—it will require reimagining care through the lenses of vision, trust, adaptability, and human-centered design. Visionary leaders must go beyond operations and drive transformation at the cultural, technological, and strategic levels.

What This Book Delivers

Narrative-Driven Leadership Insight: Deep storytelling meets healthcare strategy in a way that's both practical and inspiring.

Original Strategic Models: Five proprietary frameworks, including:

- The VISION Framework
- The Strategic Elasticity Grid
- The Culture-as-OS Canvas
- The Signal Scanning Radar
- The Legacy Loop

Future-Focused Thinking: Realistic 2045 healthcare scenarios to inform strategic foresight and investment.

Scalable Application: Designed for use in health systems, provider groups, and strategic retreats.

Who This Book Is For

- Health system CEOs and COOs
- Strategy, innovation, and operations leaders
- Clinical executives navigating digital transformation
- Policy influencers and transformation consultants

Why This Matters Now

The era of "wait and see" in healthcare leadership is over. Visionary leaders are needed—not only to interpret change but to initiate it.

"I don't just study change—I build what comes next."

- Sumit Sharma

About the Author

Sumit Sharma, MBA, FHFMA, SCPM, SSMBB, is a nationally recognized healthcare strategist and transformation leader with over 20 years of experience spanning hospital operations, service line growth, and enterprise-level innovation. He works an executive leadership role for a large healthcare organization in Phoenix, Arizona. He brings a rare blend of strategic foresight, operational fluency, and human-centered leadership to the most pressing challenges in modern healthcare.

Sumit holds a Master of Business Administration focusing on healthcare strategy and finance. He is a Fellow of Healthcare Financial Management Association (FHFMA), Stanford Certified Project Manager (SCPM), a Certified Healthcare Financial Professional (CHFP), and a Six Sigma Master Black Belt (SSMBB). He has also completed Stanford's Artificial Intelligence (AI) Specialization in Healthcare program, equipping him to bridge advanced technologies with enterprise strategy, clinical operations, and system transformation.

Sumit is the author of multiple books on operating room efficiency, healthcare leadership, and future-ready system design. His work has influenced senior executives and care delivery teams nationwide, and he is frequently invited to speak on visionary leadership, innovation scaling, and value-based system design.

What sets Sumit apart is his ability to connect the dots between vision, strategy, technology, operations, people, and sustainable impact—always in service of building a better, more humane future for patients and providers alike.

Visit: www.sharmxleadership.com

Forward

By Scott Becker

Founder and Publisher, Becker's Healthcare

In a time of immense pressure and rapid transformation, healthcare demands a new kind of leadership—one that is strategic and deeply human. The Visionary Edge meets that moment with clarity, courage, and practical insight.

Sumit Sharma brings to this book both a sharp strategic mind and a deep understanding of the daily operational realities healthcare leaders face. His writing weaves together future-focused thinking with grounded examples, making this work a valuable companion for executives, clinicians, and innovators across the industry.

What stands out most is the book's balance—it offers vision without abstraction and strategy without jargon. Sumit challenges us to rethink leadership in an AI-enabled world, design systems that center patients without losing efficiency, and embrace change with integrity.

It's easy to talk about transformation. It's much harder to map out how to get there. The Visionary Edge does just that—and does it well.

I'm honored to offer this foreword and encourage healthcare leaders to engage with this timely, thoughtful work at every level.

Scott Becker

Founder, Becker's Healthcare

Acknowledgments

Writing this book was more than a creative endeavor—it was a personal journey grounded in purpose, fueled by conviction, and shaped by those who continually inspire me to lead boldly.

To my parents, Prof. Dr. Meena Sharma and Mr. V.N. Sharma, IPS, thank you for instilling the discipline to persevere and the compassion to lead. Your example is my foundation.

To my wife, Deepti, your unwavering support and quiet strength make everything I pursue possible. You are the anchor that steadies every storm.

To my children, Savar, Saesha, and Vyom, your curiosity, laughter, and questions keep me grounded in the future. I hope to help shape you and your generation.

To my brother, Varun Sharma, and my sister, Dr. Bulbul Salwan—thank you for always supporting me. Your encouragement has meant more than words can say.

To my mentors and colleagues over the years—thank you for challenging my thinking, expanding my vision, and believing in the impact of this work. You've helped turn ideas into action.

And to every leader in healthcare trying to build something better—not just faster or cheaper, but more human—I see you. This book was written for you.

Let this work signal that the future belongs to the brave, the kind, and the visionary.

— Sumit Sharma

TABLE OF CONTENTS

Prologue: The Future is Closer Than You Think

The year was 2045, but for Sarah, it felt like she had stepped into a different universe. As she walked into the sprawling healthcare campus, glass walls shimmered with embedded data streams, reflecting key patient trends and performance metrics. Digital assistants hovered beside staff, their holographic forms relaying urgent updates. Patients entered without paper forms were seamlessly identified through biometric scans that matched their records to their digital health profiles.

However, the most remarkable change wasn't the technology but how healthcare leaders operated. Decision-making felt precise yet empathetic. Strategic plans stretched across decades, not quarters. Bias had been replaced with objective analysis. The system didn't just react to illness — it anticipated it, preventing crises before they began.

Sarah had seen this transformation unfold firsthand. She had spent the past two decades building a healthcare system that combined technology with deeply human leadership values. Gone were the days when hospitals scrambled to adjust to industry disruptions; instead, they had been guided by leaders who envisioned the future and acted decisively. These leaders didn't just adapt — they shaped the landscape itself.

But Sarah knew this evolution hadn't come easily. The early 2020s had been chaotic — hospitals facing capacity crises, burnout crippling healthcare teams, and technology advancing faster than leaders could manage. Mistrust of data systems, resistance to automation, and organizational inertia had held back progress.

Sarah's journey began during those uncertain times. As a mid-level manager in 2025, she had seen her hospital hesitate to adopt predictive analytics, fearing backlash from staff who worried algorithms would replace them. But the actual turning point came when Sarah's mentor, a visionary CEO, challenged her:

"The leaders who will thrive," he had said, "aren't the ones who react fastest — they're the ones who prepare their teams before the storm hits. If you want to lead, Sarah, you must see the future before anyone else."

That challenge changed everything. Over the years, Sarah learned to harness data for precision and foresight. She built teams that embraced innovation without losing their sense of compassion. She saw how leaders who confronted bias in decision-making — embracing what she called Zero Perception — achieved outcomes that were more equitable, effective, and trusted by patients and teams alike.

Now, standing at the heart of a transformed healthcare system, Sarah understood that authentic leadership wasn't about technology alone — it was about seeing past the immediate horizon and shaping healthcare for generations to come.

This book is about leadership that anticipates, adapts, and acts purposefully. It's about building healthcare systems that embrace the future without losing their human core. For leaders willing to embrace this mindset, the future isn't something to fear — it's an opportunity to lead with courage, vision, and purpose.

Welcome to The Visionary Edge.

Chapter 1: The Future Unfolds – Healthcare Leadership in 2045

Section 1: The Next Horizon – What Healthcare Will Look Like in 2045

The year 2045 may seem distant, but for those shaping healthcare today, it's much closer than it appears. Healthcare leaders in this future won't just manage hospitals or medical practices — they will guide entire care ecosystems. As the population ages, chronic conditions rise, and artificial intelligence matures, leadership will demand a bold shift from reactive management to proactive vision.

Imagine standing at the entrance of a healthcare campus in 2045. The traditional hospital structure has evolved. Instead of overcrowded ERs and busy waiting rooms, care is decentralized. Remote patient monitoring systems detect early warning signs before emergencies, prompting proactive intervention. Patients no longer passively visit doctors — they engage in real-time conversations with digital care advisors and health coaches. Physicians, pharmacists, nutritionists, and mental health experts collaborate across digital platforms to deliver unified care tailored to each patient's needs.

The most significant change isn't just in the tools — it's in the mindset of healthcare leaders. These leaders don't just manage clinical operations; they anticipate trends, create strategic roadmaps, and inspire organizations to act boldly in the face of disruption. Healthcare in 2045 belongs to those who can blend strategic foresight with empathy, data, and innovative thinking.

A World of Predictive Care

In 2045, preventive medicine is the default approach to care. The role of primary care has expanded, shifting from routine checkups to highly individualized care strategies driven by AI diagnostics and real-time data. Predictive algorithms anticipate chronic conditions long before symptoms appear, allowing care teams to intervene proactively. Genetic insights, lifestyle monitoring, and environmental data are synthesized to personalize treatment plans drastically.

For example, consider an individual named Alex. Years before developing hypertension, Alex's digital health assistant detects minor fluctuations in blood pressure patterns. Combined with sleep data and nutritional logs, the system identifies early warning signs. Alex's physician is alerted automatically, prompting a lifestyle intervention plan that prevents the condition from escalating. This predictive care model prevents costly interventions and improves patient outcomes through early action.

But Alex's story is not isolated. In rural communities, predictive care has become a transformative tool for addressing gaps in access. Another example is Maria, a mother of three living in a remote town with limited access to specialists. For years, Maria struggled to manage her diabetes due to inconsistent follow-ups. By 2045, digital health hubs with AI-driven triage systems changed her reality. A remote monitoring device flagged her fluctuating glucose levels, prompting a virtual consultation with an endocrinologist 200 miles away. The doctor adjusted her medication in real time, preventing a dangerous diabetic episode. Maria's story is one of many where predictive care eliminates delays and improves outcomes.

The Decentralized Hospital

By 2045, healthcare delivery will have expanded beyond centralized hospitals. Care will be delivered across integrated networks where patients receive treatments at satellite clinics, specialized centers, and even in their homes. Digital command centers will track patient populations across multiple locations, allowing medical teams to make real-time data-driven decisions.

For example, heart failure patients at risk of hospitalization may receive daily vitals monitoring through wearable sensors. If early signs of fluid retention emerge, digital triage teams will coordinate telehealth visits, medication adjustments, or in-home nursing support — all before the patient feels unwell enough to visit the ER.

For families managing pediatric conditions, decentralized care has been life changing. Emma, a 7-year-old with severe asthma, no longer requires frequent hospital visits. Sensors in her home monitor air quality, pollen levels, and medication compliance. Her parents receive alerts when environmental triggers are detected, and a telehealth team guides them through immediate interventions. What was once a constant cycle of ER visits has transformed into a proactive care model that empowers families to manage complex conditions.

AI as the Decision-Making Partner

In 2045, AI won't replace human leaders, but it will become an indispensable advisor. Predictive systems will assess vast data sets, flag risks, and recommend proactive strategies. Healthcare leaders will rely on these insights to guide resource allocation, workforce planning, and clinical protocols.

For example, an AI system may predict an upcoming flu surge two weeks in advance in a primary metropolitan hospital system. With this insight, healthcare leaders can redirect staffing resources, expand vaccine distribution, and adjust elective surgery schedules — mitigating the crisis before it fully emerges.

AI will also empower frontline staff. Intelligent care assistants will recommend prioritization strategies for nurses managing complex patient loads. By analyzing each patient's condition, medication needs, and risk level, these systems will help nurses manage their time more effectively — ensuring urgent needs are addressed without compromising care quality.

The New Role of Healthcare Leaders

In this fast-changing environment, the role of healthcare leaders will be redefined. The most successful leaders will embrace adaptability, combining strategic vision with the courage to challenge traditional thinking. They will focus on improving clinical outcomes and shaping systems that empower patients, engage communities, and foster resilience.

Healthcare leaders will need to think like futurists — anticipating shifts in demographics, technology, and social trends — while anchoring their decisions in values prioritizing patient well-being. The future won't be built by those who cling to outdated models; it will belong to those bold enough to create it.

For example, organizations that thrived in the late 2020s often credited their success to forward-looking leadership. These leaders didn't just adopt technology — they embedded innovation into their culture. Hospitals that shifted from fee-for-service models to proactive care pathways achieved lower readmission rates and higher patient satisfaction. Future leaders will embrace this same mindset — redefining what it means to lead in healthcare by designing systems that predict, prevent, and personalize care.

Section 2: Navigating Healthcare's Cultural Shift in 2045

Five Elements That Make Innovation a Daily Habit

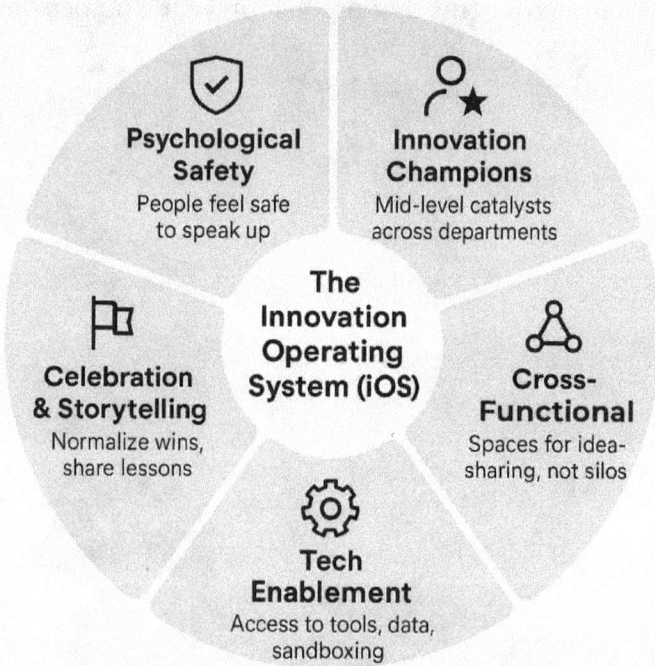

Psychological Safety
People feel safe to speak up

Innovation Champions
Mid-level catalysts across departments

The Innovation Operating System (iOS)

Celebration & Storytelling
Normalize wins, share lessons

Cross-Functional
Spaces for idea-sharing, not silos

Tech Enablement
Access to tools, data, sandboxing

By 2045, healthcare will have experienced a profound cultural shift that demands innovation and a complete redefinition of leadership. While technology will significantly improve clinical outcomes, the cultural changes within healthcare organizations will ultimately determine whether leaders succeed or fail. Future healthcare leaders must recognize that the most transformative shifts won't come from algorithms or automation — they will emerge from the mindsets, behaviors, and values that define healthcare teams.

A Culture of Proactive, Patient-Centered Care

In 2045, the most successful healthcare organizations will have eliminated the reactive mindset that defined earlier decades. Gone are the days when leaders managed crises as they unfolded. Instead, healthcare systems will be built around prevention, prediction, and early intervention. This shift demands a fundamental cultural change that repositions healthcare staff as proactive stewards of wellness rather than responders to illness.

Consider the story of Jefferson Medical Center, a large academic hospital that struggled with excessive emergency room visits in the 2020s. Patients frequently sought urgent care because they lacked access to routine preventive services. Recognizing this pattern, Jefferson's leadership team committed to transforming its culture. They shifted their mindset from "treating problems" to "anticipating needs."

By 2045, Jefferson's emergency visits had declined by 40%. The organization invested heavily in community-based outreach teams, partnering with schools, churches, and neighborhood organizations. They deployed mobile health units to underserved communities and implemented predictive analytics to identify patients at risk of chronic conditions. Staff no longer viewed patient visits as isolated transactions — they became ongoing partnerships rooted in education, prevention, and trust.

This transformation succeeded because Jefferson's leaders recognized that a cultural shift was necessary — one that empowered employees at all levels to see their role as proactive caregivers rather than reactive responders.

Breaking Silos — The Rise of Collaborative Leadership

Healthcare systems in 2045 are no longer organized into rigid, isolated departments. Instead, interdisciplinary collaboration has become the backbone of effective care delivery. Successful leaders must cultivate environments where physicians, nurses, pharmacists, social workers, and data scientists collaborate freely to improve patient outcomes.

For example, the Mayo River Valley Health Network, a significant healthcare system serving rural populations, revolutionized its care model by forming "Care Ecosystem Teams." Each team included clinical staff, data analysts, social workers, and public health experts. Rather than relying on isolated handoffs between departments, these teams met regularly to review patient populations, evaluate data trends, and design interventions that proactively improved outcomes.

As a result, Mayo River Valley's patient readmissions dropped by 30% over five years. More importantly, staff morale improved as employees found more significant purpose and clarity in their roles. The lesson was clear: healthcare leaders in 2045 must break down traditional silos and build cultures that foster collaboration, data-sharing, and collective problem-solving.

Psychological Safety as a Leadership Imperative

The most effective leaders in 2045 will understand that innovation thrives in environments where employees feel safe to speak up, offer ideas, and question assumptions. The ability to challenge the status quo without fear of punishment will be a defining feature of future-ready healthcare organizations.

Consider the example of Horizon General, a multi-specialty medical center that struggled with chronic delays in surgical workflows. In the past, staff avoided raising concerns about procedural inefficiencies, fearing backlash from senior leaders. Recognizing the need for cultural change, Horizon's new CEO implemented a "Challenge First" policy. Staff were actively encouraged to propose workflow improvements, and leaders celebrated — rather than criticized — frontline employees who challenged inefficient processes.

Over time, this cultural shift dramatically improved operational efficiency. OR turnover times improved by 18%, and Horizon's staff engagement scores climbed to the 95th percentile. Future healthcare leaders must embrace this mindset, recognizing that true innovation emerges when employees feel safe to voice ideas, even if those ideas challenge deeply held norms.

Redefining Success — Beyond Traditional Metrics

By 2045, healthcare leaders will measure success by clinical outcomes and the strength of relationships they foster — with employees, patients, and communities. Leading organizations will focus on creating meaningful human connections alongside technological advancements.

The University of Pacific Health System illustrates this shift. By 2045, they had integrated "Community Impact Scores" into their organizational dashboard, evaluating success based on preventive care rates, community wellness initiatives, and social equity outcomes. Their CEO described this change as "leading with compassion as much as data." The organization's financial strength grew steadily, but its most significant achievement was building a culture that connected care teams directly to the communities they served.

This cultural shift allowed the University of Pacific to recruit and retain top talent. In an increasingly competitive market, leaders realized that creating purpose-driven work environments was just as vital as adopting cutting-edge technology.

Embracing Cultural Change as a Leadership Discipline

The most successful healthcare leaders in 2045 will be those who understand that culture isn't simply an organizational trait — it's a strategic asset. Leaders who invest in psychological safety, foster collaboration, and measure success beyond financial metrics will shape organizations that thrive in an unpredictable future.

The challenge for leaders today is building this cultural foundation that redefines care as proactive rather than reactive, encourages interdisciplinary collaboration, and places psychological safety at the heart of innovation. Healthcare's future belongs to those who embrace cultural change as a leadership discipline — not just a managerial priority.

Section 3: The Evolution of Leadership in 2045 — The Mindset Shift That Redefined Healthcare

Hierarchy	Health Ecosystem
Rigid, top-down structure	Regenerative, distributed network
Centralized control	Decision-making at the edges
Siloed functions	Cross-disciplinary teams
Static + linear	Adaptive + dynamic

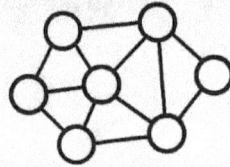

The healthcare leaders of 2045 did not emerge overnight. Their influence was forged through hard-fought battles — navigating rapid technological change, overcoming resistance to innovation, and redefining what it means to lead in complex healthcare ecosystems. By 2045, the most successful leaders will have shifted away from the traditional command-and-control style of lean leadership style with adaptability, empathy, and long-term vision.

This evolution wasn't easy. Many organizations that clung to outdated leadership models — those that relied on rigid hierarchies, top-down control, or reactive decision-making — found themselves unable to survive. Meanwhile, those who adapted thrived by embracing five key mindset shifts that redefined healthcare leadership in 2045.

1. From Manager to Visionary — The Shift to Long-Term Thinking

In 2045, effective leaders no longer focus solely on immediate results. Instead, they prioritize long-term strategy, investing in innovations that may take years to bear fruit. These leaders see beyond immediate financial targets — they focus on building sustainable systems that improve patient outcomes and community well-being.

Consider the example of NovaHealth, a prominent integrated healthcare network. In the early 2030s, NovaHealth faced a financial crisis. Short-term cost-cutting measures have weakened clinical outcomes and damaged employee morale. Recognizing the need for bold action, NovaHealth's CEO, Dr. Elena Martinez, shifted the organization's strategy to focus on long-term outcomes rather than quarterly targets.

Dr. Martinez spearheaded a "Five-Year Wellness Plan," investing in preventive care infrastructure, expanding community health initiatives, and embracing AI-driven diagnostics to predict chronic conditions before they developed. While this investment strained NovaHealth's budget in the short term, the results paid off dramatically. By 2040, readmission rates had dropped by 45%, while employee satisfaction scores soared. NovaHealth became a model for how healthcare leaders could balance immediate financial needs with a broader, long-term vision.

2. From Authority to Empowerment — Cultivating Leadership at Every Level

In 2045, healthcare organizations no longer rely on singular "heroic" leaders to drive transformation. Instead, they distribute leadership across all levels, empowering frontline staff to take ownership of decision-making.

For example, the Coastal Care Network, a mid-sized hospital group, struggled with surgical delays and inconsistent discharge planning in the 2030s. Rather than issuing top-down directives, Coastal Care's leadership team empowered nursing units and surgical teams to create their solutions. Staff were given access to data dashboards that tracked patient progress, surgical delays, and care outcomes. With this information, frontline employees created process improvement strategies, reducing surgical delays by 30% and cutting post-surgical readmissions by 20%.

This cultural shift — giving power to the people closest to the problem — proved far more effective than traditional control-based leadership methods. By 2045, empowering teams to take ownership of decisions had become a standard leadership practice.

3. From Risk-Averse to Experimentation — Embracing Innovation Through Failure

In 2045, successful healthcare leaders no longer view failure as a setback but as an opportunity to learn, innovate, and improve. Innovation hubs, dedicated solely to testing new ideas, have become standard across forward-thinking organizations. These hubs create safe environments where staff can develop new protocols, test emerging technologies, and challenge established workflows without fear of judgment.

One powerful example comes from the Phoenix Valley Medical Group. Faced with a rise in sepsis-related mortality rates in the late 2020s, their leaders created a "Rapid Experimentation Lab." Staff were encouraged to test new approaches to early sepsis detection. Over two years, dozens of experimental models were trialed, generating valuable insights. One successful pilot combined wearable monitors with AI-driven alerts, notifying physicians of subtle physiological changes linked to early-stage sepsis. This innovation resulted in a 60% reduction in sepsis-related mortality.

By embracing failure as part of the innovation process, Phoenix Valley transformed itself from a reactive organization to a proactive healthcare leader.

4. From Control to Collaboration — Building Networks of Influence

By 2045, effective healthcare leaders no longer operate within organizational silos. Instead, they build expansive networks — connecting with industry partners, technology firms, community groups, and policymakers to shape healthcare's future. These collaborations allow organizations to share insights, reduce duplication, and implement best practices more efficiently.

Consider the National Oncology Network, a coalition formed in the 2030s. Recognizing that cancer care had become increasingly complex, leaders across multiple hospital systems partnered to create a shared oncology database. This database allowed oncologists to collaborate in real-time, sharing data on tumor profiles, genetic markers, and treatment outcomes. Patients no longer faced fragmented care — specialists from different institutions collaborated seamlessly to deliver personalized treatment plans. By 2045, survival rates for complex cancers had risen by 15% in regions that adopted this network model.

Future healthcare leaders must embrace this collaborative mindset — leveraging collective intelligence across organizations to improve care at scale.

5. From Data-Driven to Data-Informed — Balancing Analytics with Emotional Intelligence

While data analytics will significantly shape healthcare in 2045, successful leaders will recognize that data alone cannot replace empathy, intuition, and emotional intelligence. Healthcare is still a profoundly human profession; leaders must balance analytical precision with compassion and understanding.

One standout example comes from MercyHealth Arizona. After implementing a comprehensive AI-based diagnostic platform in the early 2040s, MercyHealth's leadership recognized that patients felt alienated by the highly automated care model. Leaders introduced a "Human First" policy that required all clinical teams to blend data insights with relational care strategies. Physicians were trained to explain AI recommendations in language patients could understand, while nursing teams practiced empathy-driven communication to improve emotional connection.

This balance between data-driven insights and compassionate leadership resulted in a 30% improvement in patient satisfaction scores, reinforcing the power of human connection in a data-driven world.

The Leader of 2045 — A New Profile Emerges

By 2045, the most effective healthcare leaders will combine these five mindsets shifts to create resilient, forward-looking organizations. They will inspire teams to embrace innovation without losing sight of human values. They will empower frontline staff while maintaining a strategic focus on long-term outcomes. Most importantly, they will see leadership not as a position of power but as an opportunity to shape the future of healthcare for generations to come.

Zero Perception Leadership
From Fog to Clarity

Fog of Assumptions

Assumptions
Bias
Legacy Thinking
False Certainty

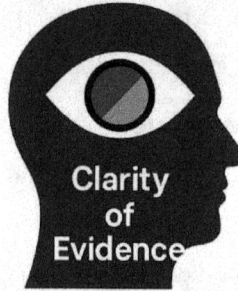

Clarity of Evidence

Insight
Inclusion
Real-Time Feedback
Belief

Section 4: Leading Through Disruption — How Healthcare Leaders Overcame the Challenges of Change

Healthcare's transformation into a predictive, proactive, and personalized system did not come without disruption. By 2045, leaders will have learned that navigating disruption isn't about avoiding uncertainty but learning to thrive. Successful healthcare leaders will have developed the capacity to manage instability while inspiring teams to remain focused on long-term vision and values.

The path to transformation was difficult. As digital tools advanced, AI systems replaced many traditional roles, and patients demanded more significant involvement in their care; healthcare leaders faced a perfect storm of workforce resistance, cultural barriers, and operational instability. Those who succeeded learned to embrace three key strategies for leading through disruption: adaptability, transparent communication, and purpose-driven resilience.

Adaptability — Thriving in an Era of Constant Change

By 2045, adaptability became essential as healthcare systems faced wave after wave of disruption — from rapid advances in diagnostic technology to shifting government regulations and evolving patient expectations.

Consider the case of Horizon Northwest Health, a multi-site healthcare system on the brink of collapse in the early 2030s.

Advances in telemedicine have made their traditional hospital-centric model unsustainable. Patients now demanded more decentralized care models, yet Horizon's leadership team resisted change, clinging to outdated practices that kept care delivery confined to their main campus.

Recognizing the urgent need for change, Horizon's new CEO, Dana Patel, introduced a rapid adaptability framework. Patel created cross-functional "response units," where clinical teams, IT leaders, and data analysts worked collaboratively to address emerging challenges. These units developed a flexible staffing model that expanded telehealth services, implemented digital prescription renewals, and created virtual follow-up clinics. By 2045, Horizon had transformed from a stagnant healthcare provider into a model of decentralized care innovation.

Patel's lesson was simple yet powerful: adaptability must be cultivated through structured innovation — empowering teams to adjust workflows, test new strategies, and learn from failure without hesitation.

Equally important, adaptability requires leaders to invest in workforce training. Patel's leadership team implemented "Rapid Skills Rotation," a cross-training program where employees rotated between clinical, technical, and administrative roles. This expanded their ability to shift seamlessly between care settings, reducing the risks of workforce burnout and improving operational flexibility.

Additionally, Patel's team created a "Change Champions" program that empowered select employees to become advocates for innovation. These champions became critical voices during transitions — coaching peers, addressing concerns, and reinforcing Horizon's evolving mission. As a result, adaptability became embedded in the organization's DNA, positioning Horizon to grow alongside the healthcare landscape.

Transparent Communication — Building Trust in Times of Uncertainty

In an era where data-driven insights and AI influence clinical decisions, leaders must build trust by embracing transparent communication. Future healthcare leaders will understand that silence in times of disruption breeds fear and resistance. Clear communication, even when conveying brutal truths, will define resilient organizations.

An inspiring example comes from Crestview Medical Center, which faced widespread resistance when introducing predictive analytics to guide clinical decision-making in the late 2020s. Physicians feared algorithm-driven care would reduce autonomy, while nursing teams worried about job displacement. Instead of pushing forward without dialogue, Crestview's leadership team prioritized transparency.

They hosted a series of "Insight Forums" — open conversations where staff could voice concerns, challenge data models, and understand the intended role of predictive insights. These forums allowed leaders to address misunderstandings head-on. They clarified that AI was designed to guide, not replace, clinical judgment. As a result, employees felt empowered to engage with the new system, and predictive models improved clinical outcomes across the organization.

Crestview's leadership also introduced a "Decision Clarity Board" — a real-time digital dashboard displaying key organizational decisions, rationale, and expected outcomes. Crestview fostered greater trust and alignment by giving employees visibility into leadership reasoning.

By 2045, Crestview's success became a widely studied example of how transparent communication can turn fear into trust — transforming resistance into alignment.

Purpose-Driven Resilience — Keeping Teams Grounded in Values

In times of disruption, the most effective healthcare leaders ensured their teams remained grounded in shared values. By 2045, organizations that weathered disruption successfully had embedded purpose into every aspect of their culture. Leaders cultivated resilience by anchoring their organizations to a meaningful mission — reminding teams why they entered healthcare in the first place.

Take the case of St. Mary's Care Network, a faith-based system facing economic instability in the 2030s. As budget constraints forced layoffs and restructuring, employee morale plummeted. Nurses, physicians, and frontline staff reported emotional exhaustion. St. Mary's leadership redefined its mission to recognize the need to restore purpose, shifting from "delivering excellent care" to "transforming lives through healing and compassion."

Leaders introduced regular "Purpose Conversations," where frontline staff shared stories of lives they had impacted. They reinvested in community outreach, creating mobile units that served underserved populations. Employees found renewed meaning in their roles, and engagement levels rebounded. In 2045, St. Mary's had stabilized financially and grown into a respected leader in community-based care.

Additionally, St. Mary's introduced "Resilience Labs," small group discussions where staff could process stress, exchange coping strategies, and strengthen their sense of purpose. These sessions, facilitated by counselors and peer leaders, equipped employees with emotional resilience tools that sustained them during turbulent periods.

The lesson was clear: in times of disruption, leaders who anchor their organizations to purpose create teams that can endure instability without losing focus.

The Leadership Blueprint for Thriving in Disruption

By 2045, leaders who successfully navigated disruption embraced three guiding principles:

- Embrace change as an Opportunity: Instead of resisting disruption, they viewed instability as a chance to refine processes, improve outcomes, and unlock new opportunities.
- Create Channels for Transparent Dialogue: Successful leaders engage employees by building trust, addressing anxieties, and ensuring clarity in times of uncertainty.
- Ground Every Decision in Purpose: Leaders who anchored their teams in meaningful values fostered resilience, ensuring employees remained focused and motivated during challenging transitions.

Additionally, effective leaders adopted "Disruption Drills" — simulation exercises where healthcare teams practiced responding to crisis scenarios such as data breaches, supply chain failures, or system outages. These proactive drills helped teams identify vulnerabilities, refine protocols, and build confidence in navigating unexpected disruptions.

The leaders of 2045 were not those who avoided disruption — they were the ones who embraced it, transforming uncertainty into an opportunity for meaningful progress.

Section 5: The FORESIGHT Model — A Leadership Framework for the Future of Healthcare

Healthcare's transformation into a predictive, proactive, and personalized system didn't happen by chance — it emerged from bold leadership decisions made years earlier. The leaders who succeeded in this evolving landscape embraced a forward-thinking mindset, blending strategy, adaptability, and compassion. To help leaders chart this path, I've developed the **FORESIGHT Model**, a strategic framework designed to guide healthcare leaders as they shape the future of care.

FORESIGHT Model
FUTURE-READY HEALTHCARE LEADERSHIP

F	Future-Focused Vision
O	Organizational Agility
R	Resilient Culture
E	Ethical Innovation
S	Stakeholder Collaboration
I	Inclusive Leadership
G	Growth-Driven Strategy
H	Human-Centered Leadership
T	Technology Integration

SHAPING HEALTHCARE'S FUTURE THROUGH VISION, HUMANITY, AND INNOVATION

The **FORESIGHT Model** is built on eight essential pillars that empower leaders to anticipate change, navigate uncertainty, and design healthcare systems that thrive in a complex world. Each element reflects the mindset and behaviors that distinguish future-ready leaders.

F: Future-Focused Vision

Leaders of the future didn't wait for trends to unfold — they anticipated them. Future-focused leaders commit to long-term strategic thinking, shaping their organizations based on predicted trends in technology, patient behavior, and care delivery models.

For example, Sunrise Valley Health recognized in the early 2030s that remote and decentralized care would dominate healthcare. Rather than resisting this shift, their leadership team invested heavily in virtual care platforms, digital diagnostics, and AI-enabled treatment plans. While competing hospitals struggled to adapt, Sunrise Valley led the way by transforming its primary care system into a hybrid model, combining in-home monitoring, telemedicine, and mobile health hubs. In the future, their proactive investments ensured they became one of the most accessible healthcare systems in their region.

O: Organizational Agility

By 2045, successful organizations no longer rely on static operating models. Instead, they adopt adaptable frameworks that allow them to shift resources, strategies, and care pathways quickly. Organizational agility becomes essential when systems face emerging crises or technology disruptions.

Consider Horizon Valley Health, a system successfully adopted during the global "Telehealth Shift." As telemedicine surged, Horizon Valley restructured its workforce to support virtual care models better. They retrained administrative staff as telehealth navigators, ensured clinicians could seamlessly transition between in-person and virtual visits, and leveraged AI to guide staffing decisions. Horizon Valley's ability to pivot quickly became a defining competitive advantage.

R: Resilient Culture

Healthcare organizations that thrived in the future shared a common trait — a deeply resilient culture built around adaptability, collaboration, and purpose. Resilient cultures empower staff to make decisions, challenge assumptions, and embrace new ideas without fear of judgment.

A powerful example emerged at Central Ridge Medical Center. After a major cybersecurity attack, the organization faced significant disruption. Patient data was compromised, workflows stalled, and trust in leadership wavered. Recognizing the need for a cultural reset, their CEO implemented a "Resilience Council." This group — composed of nurses, physicians, IT specialists, and community leaders — became the driving force behind the organization's recovery strategy. By empowering frontline teams to develop security protocols and training systems, Central Ridge rebuilt trust and emerged more potent than ever.

E: Ethical Innovation

Ethical leadership has become a crucial pillar of success in an era defined by AI, data, and automation. The leaders who shaped the future of healthcare built innovation ecosystems that balanced technological advancement with patient rights, privacy, and dignity.

For example, Westbrook Pediatrics developed an AI-based diagnostic tool to predict childhood asthma attacks. While the technology proved highly effective, the initial rollout triggered controversy when parents expressed concerns about data security. Westbrook's leadership responded by implementing transparent data policies, hosting community education events, and ensuring parents had complete control over their children's data. By embracing transparency and ethical principles, Westbrook restored public trust and achieved one of the lowest pediatric asthma rates in the region.

S: Stakeholder Collaboration

Successful leaders understood that the future of healthcare was no longer confined to hospitals — it required partnerships that crossed industries, regions, and government agencies. Healthcare leaders in this era actively engaged with community organizations, technology firms, and policymakers to improve outcomes at scale.

One standout example comes from the "Midwest Aging Alliance," a coalition formed to address the rising demand for geriatric care. Healthcare providers, senior living communities, and tech innovators joined forces to develop home-based monitoring solutions for aging populations. This collaboration improved outcomes for seniors and reduced pressure on hospitals by empowering families to manage chronic conditions at home.

I: Inclusive Leadership

The healthcare systems that flourished in the future embraced diversity at every level — ensuring leadership reflected the populations they served. Inclusive leaders encourage diverse voices in decision-making, fostering innovation by integrating ideas from cultural, social, and professional backgrounds.

At Riverbend General Hospital, leadership intentionally built diverse teams to address healthcare inequities in underserved communities. They launched mentorship programs to elevate minority leaders and recruited bilingual staff to improve communication with patients from diverse backgrounds. This inclusive leadership model became a driving force behind Riverbend's expansion into new communities, earning national recognition for health equity innovation in the future.

G: Growth-Driven Strategy

In the future, healthcare leaders will learn that sustainable growth doesn't come from short-term wins —

it requires aligning investments with long-term patient needs. Growth-driven leaders balance strategic risk-taking with financial responsibility, ensuring their organizations expand without compromising quality.

The Central Valley Health System achieved this balance by investing heavily in AI-driven diagnostics while building robust care navigation programs. This dual focus allowed them to expand services into rural regions without overburdening existing facilities. In the future, their growth model became a blueprint for expanding care without compromising standards.

H: Human-Centered Leadership

Despite advancements in automation and digital care, future healthcare leaders recognize that compassion, empathy, and emotional intelligence remain critical leadership traits. Human-centered leaders maintained strong relationships with employees, prioritized well-being, and ensured that patients experienced personalized care.

When Valley West Medical Group adopted AI-driven mental health assessments, leaders introduced "Human Touch Teams" — specialists dedicated to building emotional connections with patients. These teams complemented AI insights by ensuring patients felt heard, valued, and cared for. In the future, Valley West will become a model for balancing technology with human connection.

T: Technology Integration

Leaders in the future mastered the art of aligning technology with clinical outcomes. Rather than investing in flashy tools, they focused on integrating technology to improve safety, efficiency, and patient engagement.

Riverbend Regional Health transformed its surgical teams in Chicago by adopting AI-driven operating room systems. These tools automated surgical instrument tracking, managed sterile field protocols, and provided real-time guidance to surgeons. The result was a 32% reduction in surgical complications and a significant boost in patient safety scores.

The Power of FORESIGHT in the Future

The leaders who embraced the FORESIGHT Model didn't just manage their organizations — they reimagined them. By combining future-focused vision, adaptability, collaboration, and a steadfast commitment to ethical innovation, these leaders built healthcare systems that thrived in a world of constant change.

For today's healthcare leaders, the future isn't something to fear — it's an opportunity to shape. The decisions made now will determine whether organizations emerge more vigorous, more resilient, and better prepared to meet the needs of patients in the future and beyond.

Chapter 2: The Foundations of Future Healthcare Leadership

Section 1: Navigating Uncertainty — Why Future Healthcare Leaders Must Embrace Complexity

The future of healthcare will not unfold in predictable patterns — it will be defined by uncertainty, disruption, and rapid transformation. Leaders who thrive will be those who develop the mindset and strategies required to navigate complexity rather than resist it. The healthcare landscape will be shaped by economic volatility, technological breakthroughs, shifting workforce dynamics, and changing consumer expectations — making adaptability and foresight essential for leadership success.

The Shifting Healthcare Landscape — Forces Driving Uncertainty

Healthcare Multiple converging forces will drive healthcare's future complexity to leadership decisions. Several key megatrends will shape this new reality:

- AI-Powered Precision Medicine: Leaders must manage the integration of highly personalized treatment models driven by AI, ensuring these technologies are implemented ethically and equitably.

- Telehealth Dominance: The rise of remote monitoring, digital therapeutics, and "Hospital at Home" models will force healthcare systems to rethink facility management, staffing, and care pathways.

- Advanced Genomics and Gene Editing: Emerging tools like CRISPR will shift healthcare from reactive treatments to proactive genetic interventions, requiring leaders to anticipate ethical, regulatory, and operational implications.

- Regenerative Medicine: Innovations such as 3D-printed organs and bioengineered tissues will challenge traditional transplant pathways, forcing healthcare leaders to embrace new supply chains and surgical protocols.

- Aging Population: The growing aging demographic will increase demand for long-term care, home-based services, and chronic condition management.

- Data-Driven Ecosystems: Healthcare leaders must embrace data-sharing partnerships with insurers, pharmaceutical firms, and tech companies to ensure seamless care delivery.
- Mergers and Acquisitions (M&A): As healthcare organizations consolidate to gain scale and improve efficiency, leaders must balance integration with preserving care quality.

Future healthcare leaders must develop strategies that balance these powerful forces while maintaining stability, innovation, and patient-centered care.

The Leadership Dilemma: Balancing Stability with Innovation

In the future, healthcare leaders will face the dilemma of maintaining operational stability while driving transformative innovation. Successful leaders will recognize that these two goals are not mutually exclusive — they must learn to balance both simultaneously.

For example, consider the fictional Horizon Valley Health Network. Facing rising costs and declining inpatient volumes, Horizon Valley's leadership team recognized that continuing to expand traditional hospital services was unsustainable. Instead, they diversified by acquiring multiple outpatient surgery centers, urgent care clinics, and telemedicine startups. This blended strategy allowed Horizon Valley to stabilize its revenue while investing in future growth opportunities. By shifting resources strategically, they built a model that could adapt to evolving patient needs.

Crisis Leadership: Preparing for Unpredictable Disruptions

Future healthcare leaders must embrace crisis leadership strategies that prepare their organizations to respond rapidly to unexpected disruptions. These crises could range from global pandemics and cyberattacks to supply chain failures and economic downturns.

During the "Telehealth Surge" period, for example, many healthcare organizations experienced severe bandwidth constraints, limiting their ability to deliver virtual care effectively. While some systems struggled, Phoenix Ridge Medical Center thrived by implementing a proactive risk management framework. Leadership formed a "Disruption Readiness Task Force," which ran quarterly crisis simulation drills and partnered with telecommunications firms to expand bandwidth capacity. When the surge hit, Phoenix Ridge seamlessly scaled its virtual care services, reducing ER visits by 35% while improving patient satisfaction.

Future leaders must recognize that uncertainty isn't an occasional event — it's a constant reality. By embracing continuous scenario planning, investing in predictive analytics, and building resilient teams, healthcare leaders can prepare their organizations to thrive despite unpredictable challenges.

The Role of Mergers and Acquisitions in the Future Healthcare Landscape

As healthcare systems seek economies of scale, M&A activity will be critical in shaping future market dynamics. Healthcare leaders must master integrating acquired organizations while preserving clinical excellence and ensuring staff engagement.

Consider the example of UnityCare Health, a fictional regional system that pursued aggressive expansion by acquiring specialty clinics and ambulatory surgery centers. UnityCare's leaders faced immediate cultural resistance as newly acquired teams resisted centralized protocols. To address this, leadership launched a "Care Integration Council," composed of leaders from legacy and acquired organizations. The council identified shared best practices, created cultural exchange programs, and aligned clinical protocols. By prioritizing cultural alignment over rapid assimilation, UnityCare achieved sustained growth without compromising care quality.

Building Decision-Making Models for Complexity

In a world of volatility, healthcare leaders must adopt new decision-making frameworks that allow them to manage uncertainty without losing focus. The most effective leaders will embrace models that balance:

- Data-Driven Insights: Leveraging predictive analytics to forecast patient demand, identify care gaps, and guide resource allocation.
- Scenario Planning: Developing multiple "what-if" strategies that enable organizations to pivot rapidly in response to changing conditions.
- Cross-functional input: Engaging diverse voices — from clinicians and data scientists to supply chain experts and financial leaders — to inform strategic decisions.

For example, BrightPath Health implemented a "Dynamic Leadership Model" that required senior leaders to assess strategic risks, consider multiple response pathways, and empower frontline staff to implement localized solutions. This decentralized structure ensured BrightPath's leadership team could adjust to unexpected changes without bottlenecking decisions through a single leadership tier.

Embracing Digital Transformation in Leadership Strategy

Healthcare's growing reliance on digital systems will increase leaders' demands to build integrated technology ecosystems that improve efficiency, safety, and patient engagement. Leaders must actively guide their organizations through digital transformation without overwhelming frontline teams with complex systems.

For example, Skyline Health recognized that staff burnout increased as digital documentation systems became more complex. Leadership responded by introducing a "Digital Wellness Framework," a model that streamlined documentation protocols, automated repetitive tasks, and introduced digital support teams to guide staff adoption. By embracing digital transformation with empathy and clear communication, Skyline improved technology adoption rates and reduced clinician burnout.

Key Leadership Imperatives for Navigating Uncertainty

Future healthcare leaders must develop six essential skills to thrive in an unpredictable landscape:

1. Visionary Thinking: Leaders must anticipate trends, develop long-term strategies, and inspire teams to align with the organization's evolving mission.

2. Emotional Agility: Leaders must remain calm under pressure, demonstrating resilience and empathy during periods of instability.

3. Adaptive Execution: Leaders must translate strategic insights into flexible operational models that allow teams to pivot quickly in response to change.

4. Collaborative Leadership: Leaders must break down organizational silos, encouraging

interdisciplinary teams to co-create solutions to complex challenges.

5. Data Literacy: Leaders must become fluent in data-driven decision-making, using predictive insights to guide investment, staffing, and clinical priorities.

6. Communication Mastery: Leaders must create a transparent, honest dialogue with staff, patients, and partners to build trust during uncertain periods.

In the future, healthcare leaders will succeed by not controlling chaos but learning to lead through it. By blending strategic foresight with adaptability and resilience, they can guide their organizations through the most unpredictable challenges — shaping a healthcare system that thrives no matter what the future brings.

THE LEADERSHIP EVOLUTION LADDER

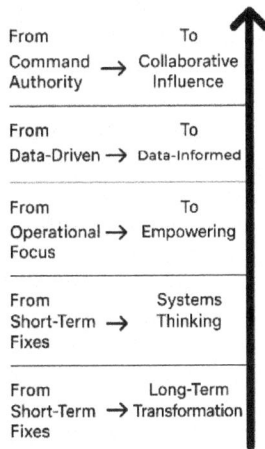

From	To
Command Authority →	Collaborative Influence
From	To
Data-Driven →	Data-Informed
From	To
Operational Focus →	Empowering
From	Systems
Short-Term Fixes →	Thinking
From	Long-Term
Short-Term Fixes →	Transformation

Section 2: Building Resilient Teams – Developing the Workforce for Future Healthcare

In a rapidly changing healthcare landscape, the ability to build and sustain resilient teams will determine organizational success. Future healthcare leaders must prepare their workforce to adapt to technological advancements, shifting care models, and economic disruptions. The most effective leaders will cultivate resilience as a crisis response strategy essential to everyday operations.

The Evolving Healthcare Workforce — Key Trends Shaping the Future

The healthcare workforce of the future will operate in an environment defined by several emerging trends:

- Remote and Hybrid Work Models: Telehealth platforms and virtual care services will redefine traditional workplace structures, requiring leaders to build remote-capable teams.

- AI and Automation Integration: As administrative tasks become increasingly automated, leaders must prepare employees to focus on strategic decision-making, critical thinking, and patient engagement.

- Aging Workforce and Skill Gaps: As older clinicians retire, healthcare organizations will face mounting pressures to fill skill gaps, particularly in nursing, primary care, and specialized fields like geriatrics.

- Mental Health and Burnout Concerns: The emotional toll of constant change will demand more substantial mental health resources, leadership support systems, and employee wellness programs.
- Flexible Staffing Models: Future healthcare leaders will rely on adaptable staffing models, leveraging gig workers, float pools, and remote specialists to manage fluctuating demand.

Creating a Resilient Workforce — Core Leadership Strategies

Building a resilient workforce requires leaders to adopt intentional strategies that empower employees to thrive amid uncertainty. Effective leaders will focus on five key pillars:

1. Emotional Resilience Training — Building Stronger Minds in the Face of Chaos

The most successful future healthcare workers will recognize that emotional resilience is not just a skill — it's a survival tool. Leaders must proactively build emotionally resilient teams that endure volatility without losing focus or morale.

For example, Horizon Valley Health introduced a "Resilience in Practice" program that provided employees with mindfulness training, cognitive-behavioral techniques, and resilience coaching. Crucially, this wasn't just a "lunch-and-learn" seminar — it was integrated into daily workflows. Staff meetings began with mindfulness exercises. Unit huddles concluded with brief reflections on stressful moments. These micro-moments built a workforce capable of withstanding uncertainty — transforming anxiety into purpose. Horizon Valley's burnout rates dropped by 40%, and staff engagement climbed to record highs.

Emotional resilience training isn't just about helping people "cope" — creating a workforce that thrives under pressure and emerges stronger with every challenge.

2. Adaptive Learning Ecosystems — Training for What Doesn't Exist Yet

The future will demand skills that haven't even been defined yet. Healthcare leaders must embrace adaptive learning models that prepare teams for change before it arrives.

Ridgeview Medical System implemented a "Learning-on-Demand" platform that used AI to recommend personalized training modules for clinical and administrative staff. Employees no longer had to wait for formal training days — the system automatically delivered micro-courses when new processes emerged. Staff absorbed knowledge in real-time, allowing Ridgeview to adopt new protocols faster than competitors. This flexible learning model empowered Ridgeview's workforce to remain agile — turning uncertainty into opportunity.

3. Empowering Frontline Decision-Making — Trusting Employees to Lead in the Moment

The days of leaders managing every detail are over. Future healthcare leaders will empower frontline teams with greater decision-making authority — giving them the tools and confidence to act without waiting for orders.

Valley West Medical Group implemented "Care Autonomy Teams," allowing nurses, technicians, and administrative staff to adjust real-time care. Staff were trained to manage complex situations without waiting for manager approval. This simple shift had profound results: patient complaints dropped, staff engagement rose, and teams reported feeling empowered rather than micromanaged. By trusting employees to make informed decisions, Valley West strengthened its workforce and improved outcomes.

4. Flexible Work Models — Balancing Stability with Freedom

The future healthcare workforce will demand greater flexibility, and leaders must meet this challenge by creating adaptive work models. Employees expect to blend on-site work with remote roles, and forward-thinking leaders will find creative ways to build agile staffing structures.

BrightPath Health developed a "FlexCare" model that gave employees control over their schedules. Some nurses worked exclusively in remote telehealth roles, others chose hybrid schedules, and support staff managed administrative tasks from home. By offering flexibility, BrightPath reduced turnover, attracted top talent, and created a happier, more stable workforce.

Flexible staffing isn't a luxury — it's the key to recruiting and retaining high-performing teams in the future healthcare workforce.

5. Investing in Mental Health Support — The Leadership Mandate of the Future

The pressure to manage continuous disruption will take a psychological toll on healthcare teams. Leaders must recognize that mental well-being is no longer a "perk" — it's a leadership priority.

Northpoint Medical Group launched "Peer Resilience Circles," safe spaces where employees openly discussed emotional fatigue, professional struggles, and personal stress. Leaders also equipped managers with tools to recognize signs of burnout, depression, and anxiety. This proactive approach created a culture where seeking help was seen as a strength, not a weakness — and staff retention improved dramatically.

Building Leadership at Every Level — Empowering the Next Generation

Future healthcare leaders won't rely on hierarchy — they'll develop leadership capacity at every level. Successful organizations will foster distributed leadership models where employees see themselves as agents of change.

Effective leaders will:

- Identify and mentor emerging leaders early, equipping them with strategic decision-making skills.
- Introduce "Leadership Pods," where multidisciplinary teams collaborate to address complex operational challenges.
- Provide rotational programs that expose employees to diverse roles, expanding their adaptability and problem-solving capabilities.

This decentralized leadership approach will empower employees to take ownership, build confidence, and embrace complexity rather than fearing it.

The Future of Workforce Well-Being — Blending Innovation with Humanity

The most successful healthcare leaders will recognize that resilience cannot be built through technology alone — it requires a deliberate focus on human connection, psychological safety, and shared purpose. By blending emotional support, flexible work structures, and adaptive learning ecosystems, leaders will position their teams to excel in the face of future uncertainty.

In the future, thriving healthcare systems will prioritize workforce well-being as much as patient outcomes. By building resilient teams today, healthcare leaders will ensure their organizations remain agile, responsive, and sustainable for years.

THE AMBIGUITY COMPASS
Navigating Leadership When the Path Isn't Clear

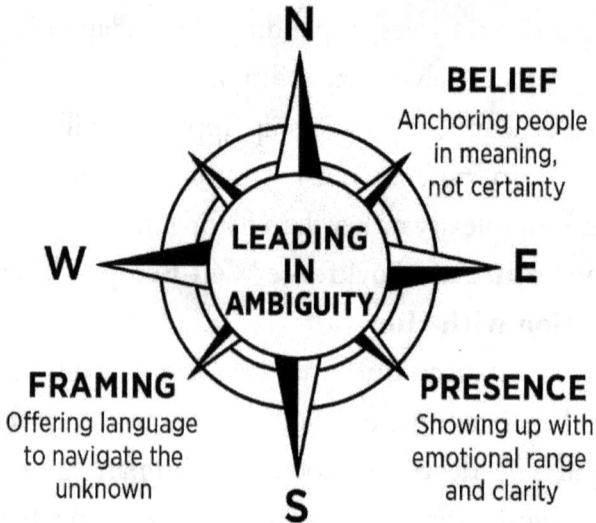

N

BELIEF
Anchoring people
in meaning,
not certainty

W

**LEADING
IN
AMBIGUITY**

E

FRAMING
Offering language
to navigate the
unknown

PRESENCE
Showing up with
emotional range
and clarity

S

Section 3: Leading with Purpose – Inspiring Healthcare Teams to Drive Meaningful Change

Healthcare leaders of the future will face a profound challenge — how to inspire teams to embrace transformative change without losing focus on the deeper purpose behind their work. The most successful leaders will recognize that purpose is the driving force that empowers teams to overcome adversity, innovate with conviction, and remain dedicated to improving patient outcomes.

Purpose-driven leadership will emerge as the defining characteristic of healthcare organizations that excel in the future. By grounding their teams in a shared mission, future leaders will foster resilience, drive engagement, and ensure healthcare professionals remain motivated amid constant disruption.

Why Purpose Matters in Healthcare Leadership

In an industry driven by clinical outcomes, financial pressures, and regulatory challenges, healthcare teams risk losing sight of their deeper "why." Purpose-driven leaders create cultures that reconnect employees to the emotional core of their work — the opportunity to improve lives, build healthier communities, and leave a lasting impact on society.

Healthcare leaders who succeed in building purpose-driven cultures will:

- Inspire employees to approach their roles with deeper meaning, reducing burnout and fatigue.
- Strengthen retention by aligning employee values with organizational goals.
- Foster innovation by encouraging staff to view challenges as opportunities to improve care.
- Build stronger connections with patients by reinforcing empathy and compassion in care delivery.

The Power of Purpose in Action — Real-World Examples

Purpose-driven leadership is not just a theoretical concept — it's a proven strategy that drives performance. Consider the example of ValleyCare Health, a multi-hospital system that faced declining staff morale after budget cuts and operational changes. Rather than focusing solely on metrics, ValleyCare's CEO launched the "Moments of Impact" initiative. Employees were invited to share powerful stories of how their work had changed patient lives. These stories were featured in team meetings, internal newsletters, and leadership updates.

The results were transformative. Employees began identifying with their impact beyond technical tasks — they saw themselves as healers, caregivers, and advocates. As a result, ValleyCare's employee engagement scores soared, and turnover rates fell dramatically within a year.

By anchoring staff in purpose, ValleyCare reinvigorated its workforce and strengthened its culture.

Embedding Purpose into Organizational Culture

Successful leaders understand that purpose cannot exist solely in slogans — it must become part of the organization's fabric. Leaders must embed purpose into their organization's values, decision-making frameworks, and performance evaluations.

To build a purpose-driven culture, leaders should:

- Redefine Success Metrics: Move beyond traditional metrics like revenue and patient throughput to include purpose-driven goals such as community impact, patient well-being, and staff empowerment.
- Share Impact Stories: Regularly highlight employee contributions that change patients' lives.
- Align Leadership Development with Purpose: Train managers to reinforce purpose in team meetings, performance reviews, and daily interactions.
- Celebrate Purpose in Milestones: Create rituals celebrating how employees' work impacts the broader healthcare mission — from successful recoveries to community outreach efforts.

Building Purpose-Driven Leaders — The Role of Emotional Intelligence

Healthcare leaders who excel at fostering purpose often display exceptional emotional intelligence (EQ). These leaders are skilled in the following:

- Active Listening: Creating safe spaces for staff to express concerns, frustrations, and aspirations.
- Empathy in Action: Demonstrating genuine concern for staff well-being and taking proactive steps to address emotional fatigue.
- Authentic Leadership: Leading by example, sharing their own "why" to inspire others to embrace purpose.

For instance, at Ridgeview Medical Group, senior leaders integrated purpose-driven dialogue into staff meetings by asking employees to reflect on a moment they made a meaningful impact. By consistently reinforcing these stories, Ridgeview's leaders created a powerful sense of belonging that improved staff retention and boosted morale during challenging periods.

Empowering Employees to Shape Their Purpose

Effective leaders recognize that purpose cannot be dictated — it must be discovered. Future-ready leaders will empower employees to shape their sense of purpose by:

- Encouraging employees to identify personal values that align with the organization's mission.

- Creating opportunities for staff to contribute ideas that improve patient care, community engagement, or workplace culture.
- Providing mentorship programs that help employees connect their career growth with their broader purpose.

For example, Evergreen Pediatrics implemented "Purpose Pods," monthly peer groups to discuss how staff could align personal values with professional goals. This initiative unlocked creative ideas for improving pediatric care and fostered deeper employee engagement.

Linking Purpose to Innovation and Growth

Purpose-driven organizations not only inspire employees — but also accelerate innovation and drive sustained growth. When employees feel connected to their "why," they are more willing to embrace new ideas, explore unconventional approaches, and adapt to industry shifts.

Leaders can link purpose to innovation by:

- Creating "Innovation Challenges" that invite staff to propose ideas that align with the organization's mission.
- Empowering frontline teams to pilot new workflows, technologies, or care models that improve patient well-being.
- Aligning growth strategies with purpose, ensuring expansion efforts prioritize community health outcomes alongside financial goals.

For example, Sunrise Valley Health Network launched a "Purpose-Driven Innovation Lab" where staff tested new ideas to improve patient engagement. One breakthrough involved using VR therapy to reduce anxiety in pediatric patients — a direct outcome of empowering staff to innovate with purpose in mind.

The Future of Purpose-Driven Leadership

In the future healthcare landscape, organizations prioritizing purpose will outperform those relying solely on efficiency and profit. Purpose-driven leaders will create teams that endure challenges with conviction, innovate with passion, and consistently exceed patient expectations.

By embedding purpose into every facet of leadership, healthcare leaders will inspire their teams to see beyond day-to-day tasks — shaping a future where healthcare isn't just about treatments but about transforming lives.

Section 4: Driving Innovation — Building a Culture of Creativity in Healthcare Leadership

In a future healthcare landscape defined by rapid technological advancements, shifting consumer demands, and disruptive care models, innovation will be the differentiator between organizations that thrive and stagnate. The most effective healthcare leaders will cultivate environments where creativity flourishes, empowering teams to develop bold ideas that improve care delivery, expand access, and enhance patient outcomes.

Healthcare innovation will no longer be confined to research labs and executive brainstorming sessions — it will become a mindset woven into everyday clinical, operational, and administrative processes. Future-ready leaders must build cultures where innovation is not an isolated event, but an ongoing process embraced by every employee.

The Innovation Imperative — Why Creativity is Key to Future Healthcare

In the healthcare systems of the future, innovation will be essential for:

Improving Patient Outcomes: AI-powered diagnostics, wearable health devices, and digital therapeutics will require leaders to embrace emerging technologies that enable earlier detection, better treatment planning, and enhanced recovery pathways.

Expanding Access to Care: Telehealth, "Hospital at Home" models, and remote patient monitoring will demand creative workflows that reach underserved populations and reduce health disparities.

Enhancing Operational Efficiency: Automation, predictive analytics, and machine learning will require leaders to reimagine staffing models, resource allocation, and clinical workflows.

Reducing Costs: Innovative care models will streamline processes, reduce hospital admissions, and shift care to lower-cost settings.

Creating an Innovation Ecosystem — Key Strategies for Future Leaders

Building a culture of innovation requires intentional leadership strategies that empower employees to think creatively, take risks, and test new ideas. Future healthcare leaders will succeed by adopting five core strategies:

1. Psychological Safety — Creating a "Safe to Fail" Environment

Innovation thrives when employees feel safe to share ideas without fear of judgment or failure. Healthcare leaders must foster a culture where experimentation is encouraged, and setbacks are seen as learning opportunities.

For example, Ridgewood Health System implemented an "Innovation Sandbox" program that invited frontline staff to test new workflow ideas in designated pilot units. Employees were encouraged to propose unconventional solutions, knowing that even unsuccessful attempts would be viewed as valuable learning experiences. By embracing experimentation, Ridgewood's leaders fostered a culture where staff felt empowered to challenge outdated practices and explore new methods.

To reinforce psychological safety, Ridgewood's leadership held monthly "Innovation Town Halls," where failed ideas were discussed as learning opportunities. Leaders reframed setbacks as stepping stones to future breakthroughs, giving employees the confidence to propose bolder ideas. As a result, Ridgewood experienced a 32% increase in employee-generated ideas, contributing to improved clinical workflows and more efficient documentation processes.

2. Innovation Champions — Empowering Change Agents

Future healthcare leaders will identify and develop "Innovation Champions," empowering employees at all levels to lead change efforts.

For instance, SummitCare Medical Group launched an "Innovation Advocate" program that trained selected staff to identify process bottlenecks, recommend improvements, and mentor peers through pilot initiatives. These champions became catalysts for change, transforming SummitCare's sterile supply chain, improving surgical prep workflows, and streamlining discharge protocols.

To further accelerate innovation, SummitCare introduced "Shadow Innovation Rounds," where Innovation Champions observed care delivery in real-time, identifying small but impactful changes that enhanced efficiency. This ground-level insight resulted in breakthrough ideas like optimized supply storage, faster surgical instrument preparation, and improved handoff protocols that reduced delays.

3. Cross-Functional Collaboration — Breaking Down Silos

Innovative healthcare leaders will dismantle traditional silos by fostering collaboration between clinicians, administrators, IT teams, and support staff. By uniting diverse perspectives, leaders unlock ideas that would otherwise go unnoticed.

Valley Regional Health introduced "Collaboration Hubs," spaces for cross-departmental problem-solving sessions. Nursing, IT, pharmacy, and finance teams met weekly to propose solutions for key challenges. This structure sparked innovations like automated medication delivery robots, real-time patient flow dashboards, and improved staffing models that balanced workload distribution.

Future healthcare leaders will expand this model by integrating external partnerships into collaboration hubs. Valley Regional Health recently invited startup founders, digital health innovators, and public health officials to participate in their brainstorming sessions. By integrating external insights, Valley Regional accelerated innovation — launching a remote monitoring program that reduced readmissions for congestive heart failure patients by 27%.

4. Investing in Emerging Technologies — Leading with Vision

Future healthcare leaders will strategically adopt transformative technologies that redefine care delivery. Leaders must move beyond passive adoption and actively guide their teams to embrace new tools effectively.

For example, FutureMed Hospital implemented a "Tech-Enabled Care Strategy," integrating AI-powered diagnostic platforms, robotic surgical systems, and virtual reality (VR) simulations for medical training. Crucially, FutureMed's leadership supported staff with dedicated training programs to accelerate adoption and minimize disruption.

FutureMed introduced "Tech Mentorships," pairing employees with technology specialists to build fluency in AI-driven decision support systems and remote patient monitoring tools to future-proof their workforce. This program strengthened staff confidence in leveraging new technologies, ensuring innovation adoption improved care quality and operational efficiency.

5. Celebrating Innovation — Recognizing Creative Contributions

In a fast-paced healthcare environment, innovation fatigue can undermine creative efforts. Future leaders will keep innovation alive by celebrating significant breakthroughs and minor process improvements.

Skyline Medical Center launched the "Innovator Spotlight," a monthly recognition program highlighting employees who introduced impactful ideas. Staff who improved discharge processes, streamlined documentation, or enhanced patient education received public recognition, reinforcing innovation as an everyday behavior rather than an isolated event.

To amplify these efforts, Skyline created "Innovation Journals," a digital platform where employees documented ideas, recorded progress, and reflected on challenges. This allowed employees to see how their contributions advanced patient care, strengthening motivation and engagement.

Linking Innovation to Organizational Strategy

While innovation flourishes in creative environments, future leaders must align innovation with their organization's broader strategy to maximize its impact. Effective leaders will:

- Develop "Innovation Roadmaps" that outline how emerging technologies align with clinical, financial, and operational goals.
- Introduce "Innovation Scorecards" that track the impact of creative ideas on patient outcomes, workflow improvements, and cost savings.

- Establish "Innovation Councils" that regularly assess new ideas, prioritize high-potential initiatives, and allocate resources for experimentation.

Future-Ready Leadership — Shaping a Culture of Continuous Innovation

Future healthcare leaders will embrace innovation as a daily practice, not a one-time event. They will empower frontline teams to think creatively, break down silos to encourage collaboration, and celebrate ideas that drive meaningful change.

By embedding innovation into their leadership DNA, healthcare leaders will create organizations that thrive amid disruption — shaping a future where creativity drives better care, improved access, and enhanced patient well-being.

Section 5: The Visionary Framework — Building a Leadership Model for the Future of Healthcare

THE VISIONARY FRAMEWORK

V	Vision-Centered Leadership
I	Innovation-Driven Culture
S	Systems Thinking
I	Inclusive Leadership
O	Outcome-Focused Decision Making
N	Nurturing Talent and Leadership Growth
A	Adaptive Strategy Execution
R	Resilience in Leadership
Y	Year-Round Learning and Growth

As healthcare evolves at an unprecedented pace, leaders will need a strategic blueprint to navigate complexity, inspire teams, and drive impactful outcomes. To help healthcare leaders adapt, innovate, and succeed in the future, I have developed the VISIONARY Framework — a model designed to empower leaders with actionable strategies for building resilient organizations in an unpredictable environment.

The **VISIONARY Framework** is built on nine essential pillars that reflect the qualities and behaviors required of future healthcare leaders:

V — Vision-Centered Leadership

Future leaders must develop a clear and compelling vision that aligns their organization with evolving industry trends. A strong vision provides clarity amid uncertainty and empowers teams to pursue ambitious goals with purpose.

For example, at BrightPath Medical Network, leaders recognized that telehealth and remote monitoring rapidly transformed care delivery. Instead of waiting for trends to unfold, BrightPath developed a bold vision to shift 40% of outpatient visits to virtual care within five years. By embedding this vision into strategic decisions, staff development, and patient engagement efforts, BrightPath successfully expanded access to care while lowering operational costs.

I — Innovation-Driven Culture

Successful healthcare leaders of the future will cultivate innovation by encouraging experimentation, celebrating creativity, and investing in emerging technologies.

At SummitCare Hospital, leaders implemented "Innovation Labs," where multidisciplinary teams collaborated to test new care delivery models. Staff were empowered to identify inefficiencies, propose innovative solutions, and pilot new processes. By fostering an innovation-driven culture, SummitCare reduced emergency department wait times by 28% and improved surgical throughput.

S — Systems Thinking

Healthcare leaders must embrace systems thinking to understand the interconnected nature of clinical workflows, staffing models, and resource allocation.

At ValleyWest Health, leaders introduced a "Whole System Flow Model," analyzing how care delivery across departments influenced hospital efficiency. By identifying bottlenecks in discharge planning, staffing, and equipment readiness, ValleyWest improved overall patient flow, reducing average inpatient stay lengths by half a day.

I — Inclusive Leadership

Healthcare leaders prioritizing diversity, equity, and inclusion will create more innovative, adaptable, and effective teams.

For instance, Crestwood Medical Center implemented a "Leadership Inclusion Circle" program, inviting underrepresented staff to participate in strategic planning discussions. By integrating diverse perspectives, Crestwood uncovered innovative solutions for improving access to preventive care in underserved communities.

O — Outcome-Focused Decision Making

Data-driven leadership will be critical for healthcare leaders as they balance financial sustainability with patient outcomes.

At NorthBridge Health, leaders introduced "Outcome Scorecards" to measure key performance indicators across clinical quality, patient safety, and operational efficiency.

These scorecards ensured that every strategic decision —
from technology investments to staffing changes —
directly supported improved outcomes.

N — Nurturing Talent and Leadership Growth

The most successful healthcare leaders will prioritize
mentorship, coaching, and development to prepare
emerging leaders for future roles.

At Evergreen Regional Health, leaders developed
"NextGen Leadership Pods," where promising employees
participated in skill-building workshops, scenario planning
exercises, and cross-functional collaboration projects. This
approach cultivated a new generation of agile leaders ready
to step into complex roles.

A — Adaptive Strategy Execution

Future healthcare leaders must master adaptive
strategies — adjusting tactics, resource allocation, and care
models in response to shifting industry conditions.

For example, MedBridge Health introduced an
"Adaptive Care Matrix," allowing staff to modify care
pathways in real-time based on changing patient volumes
and resource constraints. This strategy enabled MedBridge
to maintain optimal capacity during seasonal surges,
reducing staff burnout and improving patient outcomes.

R — Resilience in Leadership

Resilient leaders will develop mental agility, emotional
intelligence, and decision-making skills that allow them to
thrive amid uncertainty.

Pine Valley Medical Group created a "Resilience Academy," equipping managers and frontline staff with mindfulness techniques, conflict resolution training, and crisis response strategies. This proactive investment improved staff morale and faster recovery from operational disruptions.

Y — Year-Round Learning and Growth

Future healthcare leaders will embrace continuous learning as a foundation for success. The pace of change in healthcare will demand leaders who seek ongoing education, skill development, and industry insights.

At Phoenix Regional Health, leaders implemented "Growth Rounds," monthly sessions where managers shared emerging trends, case studies, and leadership strategies. By fostering ongoing learning, Phoenix Regional built a leadership pipeline that thrived on curiosity and adaptability.

Empowering Leaders to Shape the Future

The VISIONARY Framework is more than a checklist — it's a mindset that positions leaders to embrace change, inspire teams, and build healthcare organizations that thrive in the future. Leaders who embrace these nine pillars will gain the clarity, confidence, and creativity needed to shape the next generation of healthcare.

Chapter 3: From Strategy to Execution

Section 1: The Leadership Gap Between Vision and Execution

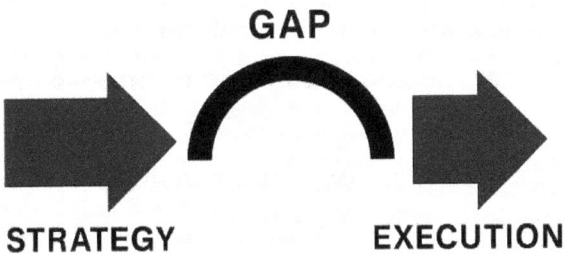

GAP

STRATEGY   **EXECUTION**

In every boardroom across healthcare today, vision decks promise transformation. They speak of digital front doors, predictive care, AI-enabled workflows, and patient-centered ecosystems. The slides are sleek. The language is bold. The intent is often sincere. Yet when you walk the hallways of the institutions that crafted those visions, you hear a different story: clinicians overwhelmed by administrative load, tech tools underutilized, patients disengaged, and innovation initiatives quietly abandoned.

This isn't a failure of ambition. It's a failure of execution. At the heart of that failure is a persistent leadership gap.

Vision is what gets leaders in the room. Execution is what earns their legacy.

The uncomfortable truth in healthcare is that many leaders have learned how to present transformation, but far fewer know how to deliver it. We celebrate crafting a five-year strategic plan, yet we don't always ask the more urgent question: how much of this will we do? How will it translate from whiteboard to workflow, from ambition to accountability?

The gap between vision and execution isn't a gap in intellect, resources, or even will. It is a gap in system design, feedback loops, ownership, and leadership follow-through. It is the space where strategy goes to stall.

In many health systems, leadership teams spend months designing strategy retreats, convening innovation councils, or creating transformation charters. These rituals have their place. However, even the best strategic roadmaps remain wishful narratives without the operational commitment to convert intention into habit. What leaders need is not more planning. They need a disciplined, adaptive, and relentlessly honest approach to execution.

Execution is not the "next step" after vision. It is the realization of the vision's worth. If vision paints the future, execution is the act of bringing it into the present.

In organizations where execution thrives, four consistent patterns emerge. These patterns don't happen by accident; they are deliberately engineered, cultivated, and reinforced by leaders who understand that strategy without execution is just theater.

1. Execution is framed as a leadership competency, not an operational task. Strategic initiatives aren't "handed off" like a baton in high-performing systems. Instead, senior leaders remain embedded in the process from concept to outcome. They ask tough questions, remove barriers, and model the urgency of delivery. Execution is treated as an executive function, not a delegated checklist item. These leaders aren't just storytellers of vision—they are architects of action.

2. The bridge between departments is deliberately engineered. Most execution breakdowns don't happen in the visioning phase. They occur in the

handoffs between strategy and IT, clinical and operational leads, and finance and innovation teams. The seams of the organization become the weak points where momentum is lost. Future-ready organizations anticipate these fractures and proactively build connective tissue—clear roles, cross-functional liaisons, standing rituals for coordination, and digital tools that ensure real-time alignment. The best leaders know that alignment is not an outcome but an infrastructure.

3. Feedback loops are fast, honest, and consequence-aware. In successful systems, dashboards are not ornamental. They are functional, accessible, and designed for decision-making. Leaders build cultures where telling the truth about performance is safe, expected, and rewarded. There are clear escalation pathways when initiatives drift off course. Instead of chasing vanity metrics or hiding failure, these organizations ask: "Are we still solving the right problem?" and "What does success look like now?" Feedback isn't retrospective; it is continuous.

4. Teams are trusted with execution and equipped for it. Empowerment is more than motivational posters and all-hands meetings. It is built into the architecture of how teams operate. Future-forward organizations invest in training, change management, decision rights, and capacity-building.

They create psychological safety and operational clarity. Teams understand the "why," own the "how," and are resourced for the "when." Micromanagement fades because alignment is structured, not improvised.

Let's look at a familiar but instructive case. A mid-sized regional health system launched a new patient engagement strategy centered around digital check-ins, automated appointment reminders, and post-visit surveys. The vision was compelling. Leadership announced it during an all-staff town hall and signed vendor contracts. However, less than 20% of patients had engaged with the system six months later. Clinicians found it cumbersome. Staff reverted to old workflows. IT was overwhelmed with troubleshooting. What happened?

There was no co-design with frontline users. No training beyond a 10-minute demo. No metrics that mattered to staff. The strategy was handed off, not handed through. This is where execution fails: leaders forget that transformation happens in the details.

Execution is where authentic leadership is forged. Leaders either retreat to old habits or rise with new clarity in the messy middle—where complexity, fatigue, and resistance live. The leaders who rise are the ones who show up, stay close, and never stop connecting vision to impact.

In the following sections of this chapter, we'll explore how to operationalize this philosophy. We'll examine the execution architecture, including prioritization frameworks, execution rituals, resource alignment, and metrics that matter. We will also study the anatomy of failed initiatives to understand what execution breakdown looks like—and how it can be prevented.

The next era of healthcare won't be shaped by what we envision; it will be shaped by what we deliver.

DEEP Execution Diagnostics

D	**Design Integrity** Is the design of the strategy internally consistent and structurally sound?
E	**Engagement Pathways** Are the right stakeholders involved and committed?
E	**Enablement Systems** Are resources, capabilities, and processes in place to enable progress?
P	**Performance Feedback** Is execution monitored, measured, and adjusted?

Section 2: Building Execution Muscle – Systems, Rituals, and Follow-Through

Execution is not a matter of willpower. It is a muscle—developed through discipline, repetition, feedback, and resilience. And just like any muscle, it can atrophy in organizations that neglect or overextend it without support. In healthcare, where leaders must navigate regulatory complexity, cultural inertia, burnout, and competing priorities, building execution muscle is not just a leadership trait but a survival strategy.

Most healthcare organizations don't fail because they lack ideas. They fail because they cannot operationalize those ideas at scale. Visionaries may light the way, but systems, rituals, and follow-through carry the weight. To build this kind of disciplined execution capability, leaders must move beyond episodic change efforts and cultivate a culture that is structurally committed to follow-through.

Systems: Building the Architecture of Accountability

Strong systems scaffold every sustainable transformation. These are not the bureaucratic, check-the-box procedures that slow innovation. Instead, they are adaptive, lean, and intentionally designed structures that support clarity, coordination, and course correction.

A robust execution system includes:

- Defined decision rights: Who owns what, who has the authority to escalate, and where accountability sits? Ambiguity here is the root of paralysis.

- Execution charters: Every initiative, no matter how visionary, must be grounded in a practical charter outlining objectives, timelines, interdependencies, and risks.

- Feedback infrastructure: Integrated dashboards, pulse surveys, and stand-up reviews that provide continuous intelligence—not just monthly retrospectives.

- Resource visibility: Transparent tracking of time, people, capital, and technology commitments to ensure strategic efforts are realistically supported.

One of the most common pitfalls in execution is underestimating the hidden toll of rework, scope creep, or cross-functional confusion. Systems are the guardrails that prevent vision from becoming a drift.

Rituals: Embedding Follow-Through into the Culture

Excellent execution is not built-in bursts—it is built-in rhythms. High-performing organizations ritualize their execution behaviors, creating recurring patterns reinforcing alignment, surface blockers, and celebrating progress.

These rituals may include:

- Weekly cross-functional syncs focused on initiative progress and priority resets.
- Monthly alignment reviews between executives and initiative lead to assess strategic traction.
- Daily or weekly stand-ups for high-velocity teams managing complex initiatives.
- Post-milestone retrospectives to build institutional learning and adapt quickly.

Rituals turn execution from an act of force into a cultural expectation. They provide predictable touchpoints where decisions are made, truths are spoken, and momentum is measured. In healthcare environments, where cognitive and emotional overload is common, rituals provide scaffolding that sustains forward motion.

One academic medical center introduced a Friday "Progress Pulse"—a 30-minute ritual where key initiative owners summarized wins, obstacles, and next steps. It was voluntary at first. Within six weeks, attendance had tripled, and the COO remarked it was the most truthful 30 minutes of the week. Why? Because ritual created permission. And permission bred ownership.

Follow-Through: Leadership's Most Underrated Discipline

Of all the execution muscles to build, follow-through is the most personal—and the most powerful. Vision without follow-through is theater. A strategy without follow-through is paperwork. In healthcare leadership's trenches, follow-through transforms insight into progress.

Follow-through looks like:

- Leaders revisit the same topic until it moves—not until the agenda changes.
- Holding one another accountable without blame, shame, or avoidance.
- Checking back in, even when results aren't immediate or easy.
- Staying the course when it gets hard, dull, or politically uncomfortable.

Future-ready leaders do not confuse delegation with detachment. They stay proximate to the work, even as they empower others to lead it. They create containers where consistency, not charisma, drives results.

The Role of Middle Management in Execution Discipline

Often overlooked in execution strategy is the role of middle managers. They are the connective tissue between vision and frontline reality. Yet they are among any healthcare organization's most under-supported and over-burdened layers.

To strengthen execution muscle system-wide, leaders must:

- Invest in mid-level leadership development: Not just how to manage people, but how to manage complexity.

- Clarify scope and authority: Middle managers need to know what decisions they can make without escalating everything upward.
- Include them in co-design: If you want buy-in, let them build the blueprint.
- Protect their capacity: Execution collapses when mid-level leaders are stretched too thin across reactive firefighting.

An integrated health system in the Midwest redesigned its project governance by including three mid-level managers in every strategic initiative steering committee. The result? Projects got more innovative, faster, and more realistic. Execution improved not because new software was installed but because the human layer of the system was seen, respected, and empowered.

Execution Fatigue: The Hidden Risk

Building execution muscle also requires recognizing when the muscle is tearing. Execution fatigue is real and often masquerades as resistance, low engagement, or performance issues.

Leaders must become fluent in reading the signs:

- Initiative overload without clear priorities.
- Excessive meeting time with no decisions made.
- Emotional exhaustion, particularly among high performers.
- Cynicism about "another strategy."

The antidote is not more pressure. It is more intelligent sequencing, clearer trade-offs, and active listening. Execution must include recovery. The best leaders embed reflection, gratitude, and breathing space into their cadence.

As one seasoned CNO said, "If everything is urgent, nothing is real. We need to let teams breathe so they can build."

Conclusion: From Muscle to Momentum

Systems create structure. Rituals create rhythm. Follow-through creates results. When these elements converge, execution muscle becomes organizational momentum.

In the next section, we will explore how to move from isolated success stories to scalable platforms—taking pilot projects and turning them into enterprise-wide transformations. Because proper execution isn't episodic, it is systemic. It is how healthcare will evolve—not through slogans or silver bullets, but through leaders who know how to build, sustain, and multiply momentum.

Section 3: From Pilots to Platforms – Scaling Innovation Across the Enterprise

In healthcare, ideas are never in short supply. What's scarce is scale. Every year, hospitals, health systems, and clinics pilot promising innovations—new care delivery models, digital tools, predictive analytics engines, and operational redesigns. And yet, far too often, these innovations remain trapped in pilot purgatory: well-intentioned, limited in scope, celebrated briefly, and then quietly shelved.

The issue isn't the failure of ideas. It's the failure to scale.

Pilots offer the illusion of progress. They demonstrate that something "can" work—but they do not guarantee that it "will" work across different service lines, regions, or patient populations. In truth, pilots are a safe space: a space to experiment, to gather data, and to reduce risk. But fundamental transformation requires what comes after the pilot—the leap from local success to system-wide adoption.

This section explores how visionary healthcare leaders build enterprise capability to turn pilots into platforms. These leaders don't just test change; they propagate it. They've mastered the muscle of scale.

The Pilot Trap: When Innovation Gets Stuck

Let's start with the trap.

A department designs a promising digital intake solution that reduces wait times by 30%. Leadership is excited. A pilot is launched in one clinic. The results are strong. Enthusiasm rises. But the expansion never happens. Why?

- The pilot was built around the talents of a few exceptional people, but it was not a scalable process.
- IT was not involved early, so integration issues emerged.
- Finance didn't allocate ongoing funding past phase one.
- No executive champion owned the scale strategy.
- Frontline staff in other departments were not consulted or prepared.

Without intentional design for scalability, even the best pilot becomes a siloed success—celebrated in newsletters but forgotten in operations.

Designing for Scale from Day One

Visionary leaders think beyond the pilot. From the beginning, they ask, "What would this look like at full scale?"

Principles of scale-oriented design include:

- Modular implementation: Build solutions so that parts can be adopted incrementally.
- Cross-functional collaboration early: Engage IT, finance, compliance, and frontline staff during the design phase.
- Policy and protocol integration: Ensure pilot practices can live within existing clinical and operational governance.

Scalability testing: Don't just test "does it work here"—test "can it travel."

One health system in the Pacific Northwest developed an AI-powered patient triage system. Instead of piloting in isolation, they launched with a "ready-to-scale" model—embedding scale pathways into their IT roadmap, budget forecasting, and workforce training. By year two, the program expanded across six regions with minimal rework.

Platforms vs. Projects: The Mindset Shift

To scale effectively, healthcare leaders must evolve from a "project mindset" to a "platform mindset."

Projects are finite. They have start and end dates, discrete goals, and localized ownership. Platforms, by contrast, are reusable infrastructures designed to support multiple innovations.

Examples of platforms include:

- A centralized digital front door framework that supports all specialties
- A typical data architecture that allows clinical AI tools to plug in across departments
- A unified care team model that enables redesign in multiple settings (e.g., ED, primary care, surgery)

When you build platforms instead of isolated solutions, each innovation adds value to the system as a whole. You stop reinventing the wheel—and start expanding the road.

Scaling Culture: Making Innovation Everyone's Job

A sustainable scale doesn't just require systems—it needs people.

Organizations that excel at scale embed innovation into their culture. They:

- Reward replication, not just originality
- Recognize leaders who adopt proven solutions with discipline
- Normalize failure as part of the scaling journey
- Use storytelling to connect the "why" of innovation across departments

One system launched a "Scale Champions Network"— a group of middle managers trained to adapt and deploy proven pilots across different markets. These champions served as internal translators, connecting the spirit of the original pilot with the realities of their local context. Adoption rates soared, not because of top-down mandates, but because trusted leaders within each team made it real.

The Role of Data and Measurement in Scaling

You can't scale what you don't measure. However, not all metrics are created equal.

Visionary leaders build measurement systems that:

- Track fidelity: Is the model being implemented as intended?
- Measure impact: Are we seeing the same outcomes in different settings?

- Surface variation: Where are we hitting resistance—and why?
- Create learning loops: What are we learning as we scale?

Too often, scaling efforts fail because success is defined narrowly. The goal isn't just to replicate metrics; it's to replicate value—and to do so in ways that honor local context.

Governance for Scaling: Who Owns the Work?

Scaling is a leadership function, not just an operational task. Without clear ownership, scaling efforts stall in ambiguity.

High-performing systems define:

- A scaling executive sponsor: Someone accountable for maintaining momentum and resolving cross-functional barriers.
- A scaling PMO (Project Management Office) or equivalent that monitors rollout, updates leadership, and coordinates resources.
- Local adaptation councils: Empowered groups who shape how the innovation is implemented locally without compromising core integrity.

This balance of central control and local adaptation is key. It's what makes the scale feel possible—not imposed.

Avoiding the Scaling Burnout

Scaling isn't just a technical challenge—it's an emotional one.

Teams may resist not because they oppose the innovation but because they feel fatigued by constant change or skeptical after seeing past pilots fade away.

The best leaders address this by:

- Acknowledging "change fatigue" openly and empathetically
- Clarifying: "Here's why this matters and how it will differ."
- Creating small wins during scale-up phases to build belief
- Protecting bandwidth: Scaling doesn't mean piling on

Healthcare professionals are not short on passion—they're short on trust that change will stick. Scaling is how leaders rebuild that trust.

Conclusion: The Architecture of Enterprise Transformation

Pilots test possibility. Platforms prove performance.

True transformation comes not from isolated brilliance but from institutional capability. The systems leading healthcare's future won't just launch great ideas—they'll scale them. They will be fluent in building structures, energizing people, and aligning resources around the hard work of scale.

In the next section, we'll examine how execution lives in data—how to lead with dashboards, decisions, and ethics in a digital-first world because scaling is not the end of execution. It's the beginning of everything else.

Section 4: The Three Gears of Strategic Execution

Every high-performing healthcare organization has its strategy on paper. Fewer have it in practice. What differentiates those who transform from those who merely aspire is not intent but infrastructure. Strategic execution is not about doing more. It's about doing the right things at the right time, with the right level of intensity.

To achieve this consistently, leaders must adopt the Three Gears of Strategic Execution: Alignment, Acceleration, and Adaptation. Like gears in a machine, these must engage with precision and coordination. When even one is missing or underdeveloped, the entire execution engine grinds or stalls.

Gear One: Alignment — Ensuring Everyone Is Aiming in the Same Direction

Alignment is the foundational gear. It ensures that people understand the strategy from the boardroom to the bedside, believe in its importance, and see their role in bringing it to life. Misalignment, even when subtle, is among the most corrosive forces in execution.

Key principles for creating strategic alignment:

- Clarity at all levels: Leaders must communicate the "what" and the "why." Clarity of purpose generates coherence in decision-making.

- Strategy cascades: Break down enterprise strategy into functional, departmental, and individual objectives with clear links.
- Eliminating shadow strategies: Ensure there is one true north. Multiple conflicting priorities create internal competition and dilute focus.
- Visual alignment tools: Strategy maps, OKRs, and balanced scorecards—used effectively—can help keep teams centered.

A health system CEO once said, "If you ask five departments what our strategy is and get five answers—we don't have a strategy." Alignment eliminates that ambiguity.

However, alignment is not a one-time event. It is a leadership discipline, a constant recalibration. It lives in town halls, project charters, and leadership huddles. Leaders must keep the strategy visible, not just as a document, but as a behavior.

Gear Two: Acceleration — Moving the Right Work Forward, Faster

Once alignment is established, momentum must follow. Acceleration is about building disciplined urgency. It's not about chaos, nor is it about speed for speed's sake. It is about removing friction, setting the pace, and generating traction where it matters most.

Acceleration requires:

- Prioritization rituals: Regularly determining what work must stop, start, or continue.

- Dedicated execution teams: Leaders must assign talent—not just tasks—to priority initiatives.
- Decision velocity: Reduce decision cycles through clear roles, delegated authority, and empowered teams.
- Removing blockers: Leaders must actively hunt and remove obstacles to progress, not wait for escalation.

An extensive Midwest health network improved its digital scheduling rollout time by 60% by redesigning its escalation pathways and empowering product teams to make real-time decisions within guardrails.

Acceleration is about rhythm. Weekly check-ins. 30-60-90-day sprint plans. Quarterly strategic reviews. The cadence of performance creates a culture of momentum.

And importantly, acceleration must be sustainable. Burnout is not a badge of honor. High execution cultures build urgency without sacrificing well-being.

Gear Three: Adaptation — Learning in Motion

No strategy survives first contact with reality. Market conditions shift. Patient behaviors evolve. Technology disrupts. That's why adaptation is the final, essential gear.

Adaptive organizations don't just execute their plans—they interrogate them. They measure, reflect, and pivot when necessary. They treat metrics not as judgment but as guidance.

The core practices of adaptive execution include:

- Learning loops: Embed rapid feedback into implementation phases.
- Strategic sensemaking: Regular sessions where teams assess external trends, internal performance, and future risks.
- Change resilience metrics: What's working and how well the organization absorbs and adapts to change.
- Scenario-based planning: Preparing for multiple futures, not just the one we hope unfolds.

Leaders in one academic health center held quarterly "strategy pulse" sessions where clinical, operational, and digital leads shared honest reflections: What's working? What's not? What assumptions no longer hold? Those conversations didn't derail execution—they deepened it.

Adaptation, at its best, is a form of strategic humility. It says: "We are committed to our outcomes, not just our path."

The Interplay of Gears: Why All Three Must Move Together

Execution fails when one gear spins without the others. Consider:

- Alignment without acceleration leads to consensus without progress.
- Acceleration without adaptation results in speed without strategy.

- Adaptation without alignment creates pivots without purpose.

Organizations that master strategic execution know how to shift gears without losing momentum. They create balance: enough structure to ensure consistency, enough flexibility to allow innovation, and enough discipline to keep the enterprise focused.

One leading integrated delivery network designed an internal "Execution Engine"—a model built on these three gears. They trained over 1,000 managers in aligning team goals to strategic pillars, built playbooks for initiative pacing, and created dashboards that guided weekly adaptive check-ins. The result? A 40% increase in initiative completion rates year-over-year and a measurable rise in staff confidence around enterprise priorities.

Building Leadership Capability Around the Gears

Execution isn't a system alone—it's a capability. Leaders must be trained, coached, and assessed on what they deliver and how they provide it. The Three Gears offer a practical leadership development framework.

- Alignment as communication competency: Can the leader inspire clarity and consistency?
- Acceleration as operational acumen: Can they drive outcomes through teams and processes?
- Adaptation as strategic agility: Can they sense shifts, respond gracefully, and lead others through change?

Future-ready leadership pipelines must embed these competencies. Promotions should consider past performance and proven ability to operate across all three gears.

Conclusion: The Gearbox of Future Execution

Execution is not luck. It is design. It is the outcome of disciplined, adaptive, and coordinated motion. The Three Gears of Strategic Execution—Alignment, Acceleration, and Adaptation—offer healthcare organizations a model for making their strategies live.

When leaders learn to manage these gears with finesse, they create systems that not only move—but move with intention, integrity, and impact.

In the final section of this chapter, we'll explore why some of the most promising strategies still fail—and what the anatomy of execution breakdown reveals about culture, accountability, and the stories organizations tell themselves about progress.

Section 5: Case-Informed Framework — Why Vision Without Execution Fails

For every breakthrough that reshapes a healthcare system, a dozen more never pass the planning stage. Strategic documents gather dust. Innovation pilots stall after early success. Workflow redesigns return to the status quo. These aren't random failures; they're symptoms of a more significant issue — the chasm between vision and execution.

This section explores why even well-designed, well-funded strategies often falter. But we don't stop at analysis. We construct a case-informed framework — a guide to diagnosing execution failures and designing systems that can carry the vision through the complexity of implementation. Drawing on real-world breakdowns and breakdown patterns, this section arms healthcare leaders with the lens they need to course-correct.

When Vision Fails to Materialize: A Pattern of Symptoms

Before we explore solutions, we must be honest about the recurring signals of execution failure:

- Initiative overload: Too many priorities competing for limited bandwidth
- Ownership confusion: Lack of clarity on who is truly accountable

- Leadership disengagement: Leaders who initiate but don't follow through
- Lack of feedback mechanisms: Progress is measured only retrospectively
- Change resistance: Frontline teams revert to old habits, unaligned with new goals
- Symbolic gestures over structural shifts: Focus on messaging rather than muscle

These symptoms are not individual shortcomings. They reflect systemic gaps in execution infrastructure and leadership culture.

Anatomy of a Failure: A Composite Case

Let's examine a fictionalized, but entirely plausible, scenario based on dozens of real-world encounters.

The Scenario: A 500-bed hospital launches a strategic plan to reduce patient length of stay by improving discharge coordination. The plan includes a new discharge dashboard, scheduled multidisciplinary rounds, and a standardized checklist for post-acute transition planning.

The Vision: More efficient throughput. Improved patient satisfaction. Reduced readmissions. Lower costs.

The Outcome After One Year:

- The dashboard is rarely used outside of three pilot units.
- Rounds occur inconsistently and without full interdisciplinary representation.

- The checklist is completed in isolation by nurses under time pressure.
- Readmission rates are unchanged.

The Postmortem:

- The discharge process was not co-designed with frontline staff.
- IT delivered the dashboard, but no training or workflow integration followed.
- Physicians received no incentive or feedback to engage.
- The initiative had no embedded metrics to measure adoption.
- Most tellingly, it was never revisited after the CEO presented the strategy in Q1.

This is not a failure of intention. It is a failure of sustained leadership, structural reinforcement, and adaptive learning. The case exposes how complex systems can quietly revert, even when goals are clear.

A Framework for Diagnosing Execution Failure

To move from insight to impact, we propose the ***DEEP Execution Diagnostic Framework:***

D – Design Integrity:

Was the initiative grounded in a real operational context?

Were end users involved in co-design?

Did the solution align with existing processes or require conflicting behaviors?

E – Engagement Pathways:

Were stakeholders (clinical, operational, IT) engaged early and meaningfully?

Was buy-in transactional or transformative?

Was there visible executive sponsorship beyond kickoff?

E – Enablement Systems:

Were teams trained to execute?

Did resources (time, technology, decision rights) support adoption?

Were workflows adjusted to accommodate the change?

P – Performance Feedback:

Were metrics relevant, timely, and visible?

Was data used to coach, not just judge?

Did leaders create regular spaces for reflection and course correction?

When any one of these dimensions is weak, execution suffers. When multiple fail simultaneously, initiatives collapse under their complexity.

Applying the Framework: A Turnaround Case

Now, let's apply the DEEP framework to a positive example.

A multi-site pediatric network sought to reduce variation in asthma management. Initial attempts failed due to low physician engagement and data fragmentation. A rebooted strategy followed the DEEP principles:

- Design: Frontline providers helped redesign clinical pathways and EHR templates.
- Engagement: Family advocates and care managers co-led the steering committee.
- Enablement: A clinical educator role was funded to support site rollouts.
- Performance: Each site had dashboards embedded in weekly team huddles, with non-punitive data transparency.

The result was a 24% drop in ED visits and a 15% increase in care plan documentation across all sites within 12 months. The difference wasn't a new idea—it was execution that respected complexity.

Extended Failure Autopsy: A National Initiative That Collapsed

In 2018, a consortium of hospitals and physician networks launched a joint effort to digitize care pathways for managing chronic kidney disease (CKD). National payers, EHR vendors, and physician groups supported it. The goal was to integrate evidence-based protocols into the clinical workflow for earlier detection and prevention.

Despite national attention and initial pilot success, the initiative disbanded by year three. Post-analysis revealed:

- No central governance structure: each region interpreted the roadmap differently.
- Physicians did not trust the alert thresholds in the EHR integration.

- Regional IT teams had different versions of software, creating inconsistencies.
- No one was accountable for scale.

The biggest lesson? Vision cannot rely on goodwill alone. Execution requires engineered alignment.

Leader Interviews: Voices from the Field

A VP of Strategy at an extensive health system shared:

"Everyone assumes the CEO will keep execution moving. But the truth is — without distributed accountability, it dies in silence."

A Chief Medical Officer reflected:

"We spent six months building a care model that never got past three floors of our main hospital. Why? Because we treated execution like a technical rollout, not a culture change."

A mid-level nurse manager said:

"I was never against the change. I didn't understand who was driving it or how it would affect my workflow. We needed fewer emails and more conversations."

These voices echo the DEEP dimensions — particularly the importance of engagement and enablement.

Organizational Storytelling and Execution

Every organization tells itself stories about why things fail. Often, they blame people. "The staff wasn't ready." "The market shifted." "The champion left." However, when we interrogate these stories, we often find that they protect the system from introspection.

Execution maturity requires cultural maturity. Leaders must create safe spaces for truth-telling. They must model curiosity instead of defensiveness. And they must normalize reflection as part of the execution cycle.

A culture of high execution maturity will regularly ask:

- What are we pretending is working?
- What's the delta between our plan and our practice?
- Where do we need to slow down to speed up?

Execution is a Narrative, Not Just a Process

In healthcare, execution is often framed as a task. But it is more than that. It is a narrative—a story we tell ourselves and others about what matters, what's possible, and what's next.

When execution fails, it's not only a missed outcome—it's a missed opportunity to strengthen identity, capability, and trust.

Conversely, when execution succeeds, even modest initiatives can reshape how people see themselves:

- Nurses become designers.
- Managers become coaches.
- Executives become sponsors, not just strategists.
- Teams become believers, not just implementers.

The ripple effects matter. Because what an organization delivers today shapes what it believes it can provide tomorrow.

Conclusion: Closing the Execution Loop

Execution failure is not inevitable. It is predictable—and preventable. By adopting structured diagnostics like the **DEEP framework**, embracing reflective practice, and anchoring leadership in sustained engagement, organizations can build resilience against the most common breakdowns.

The future of healthcare leadership is not just about vision. It is about closing the loop between vision and reality. In doing so, leaders don't just bring strategies to life—they align their organizations with their highest potential.

Execution is the bridge between today's intention and tomorrow's transformation. It begins with leaders willing to ask the more complex question: not just "What should we do?" but "What must we change to make it happen?"

Chapter 4: Leading with Data, AI, and Ethics

Section 1: Human-Machine Intelligence – Partnering with AI for Better Decisions

The future of healthcare leadership will not be written in isolation — it will be co-authored with algorithms. Artificial intelligence (AI), machine learning, and predictive analytics are no longer fringe technologies. They are central to diagnosing, monitoring, planning, and even leading. But the path to intelligent decision-making isn't about replacing humans with machines — it's about forming a strategic partnership between human judgment and machine learning.

This section examines how healthcare leaders can shape a new paradigm where human-machine collaboration becomes a strategic differentiator, not a source of confusion or fear. When leveraged wisely, AI can accelerate clinical insights, reduce administrative burden, and reveal previously invisible trends. But without thoughtful leadership, it can also amplify bias, overwhelm users, and erode trust.

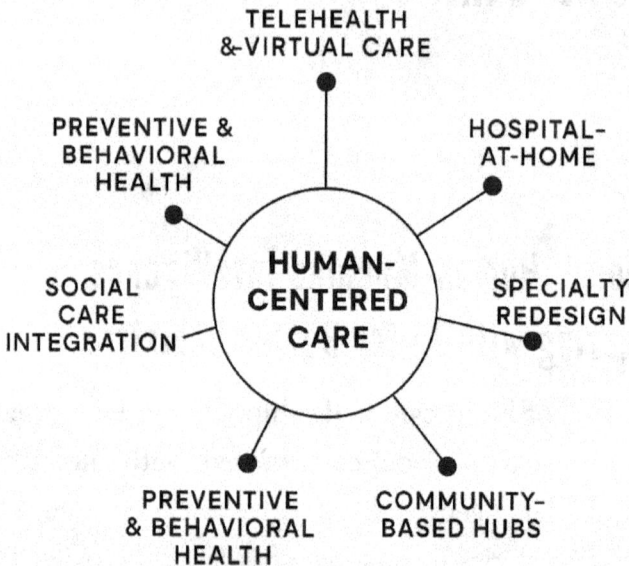

TELEHEALTH
&-VIRTUAL CARE

PREVENTIVE &
BEHAVIORAL
HEALTH

HOSPITAL-
AT-HOME

SOCIAL
CARE
INTEGRATION

HUMAN-
CENTERED
CARE

SPECIALTY
REDESIGN

PREVENTIVE
& BEHAVIORAL
HEALTH

COMMUNITY-
BASED HUBS

The stakes are high. The time for leadership is now.

Understanding the Promise and the Peril

AI has the potential to revolutionize healthcare by doing what humans cannot: rapidly process vast datasets, find non-obvious correlations, and make probabilistic predictions in real time. From early cancer detection to supply chain optimization, the impact is undeniable.

But we must hold two truths simultaneously:

- AI is **powerful** and can unlock massive operational and clinical value.
- AI is **fallible** and can scale error and inequity without careful oversight.

Healthcare leaders must embrace AI as a technology and an organizational competency. This means asking the right questions:

- What problem is this AI solving?
- Who trained the model — and on what data?
- How will it integrate into existing workflows?
- Who is accountable if the AI gets it wrong?

Moving Beyond Buzzwords: Strategic Use Cases That Matter

Not all AI investments deliver meaningful impact. Many fall into the "innovation theater" category — flashy but shallow initiatives that create excitement without value. To lead with integrity, leaders must prioritize use cases where AI supports strategic goals and enhances human capacity.

Some high-value domains include:

- Clinical decision support: AI models that assist with diagnosis, triage, and treatment pathways.

- Population health prediction: Risk scoring to prioritize interventions and allocate care management resources.
- Operational efficiency: Predictive scheduling, staffing, and bed utilization models.
- Revenue cycle optimization: Automating claim reviews, denials, and prior authorizations.
- Digital engagement: Chatbots and virtual assistants for patient communication, FAQs, and pre-visit screening.

The common denominator? Each use case augments, not replaces, human roles — freeing up cognitive space for more profound judgment and compassion.

The Role of Leadership: Creating Clarity, Not Confusion

Leaders must play three critical roles in enabling human-machine intelligence:

1. Translators and executives must be able to translate technical jargon into business implications. They don't need to code—but they must understand the basic logic of data science, how models are built, and the trade-offs involved.

2. The integrator's AI must not live in isolation. It must be embedded into workflows. This means building coalitions between clinical, technical, and operational teams — and ensuring the technology meets users where they are.

3. Stewards Leaders must ensure AI initiatives uphold ethical principles, reflect organizational values, and include diverse voices. This includes governance structures that monitor fairness, explainability, and outcomes.

Without leadership at the helm, AI initiatives become tech experiments. With leadership, they become instruments of transformation.

Trust as the Cornerstone of Adoption

The most advanced algorithm is worthless if no one trusts it. And trust in AI is not automatic — it must be earned.

Leaders must understand the psychological dynamics of adoption:

- Clinicians fear loss of autonomy or liability.
- Administrators worry about job displacement.
- Patients may distrust opaque systems they don't understand.

To build trust:

- Make AI explainable: Provide transparency into what the model is doing and why.
- Start with augmentation: Introduce AI as a second opinion, not a directive.
- Create opt-in pilots: Let users experience value before making solutions mandatory.
- Use storytelling: Share examples of how AI saved time, improved care, or prevented errors.

A Case in Leadership: Augmented Triage in Emergency Medicine

At one urban academic medical center, an AI model was deployed to assist emergency triage nurses in identifying high-risk sepsis cases based on real-time vitals and lab data.

Initial adoption was slow. Nurses didn't trust the alerts, physicians saw it as intrusive.

Leadership intervened:

- Held town halls to explain the model's logic and limitations.
- Integrated the alert into the EHR workflow, not as a popup but as a soft flag.
- Allowed nurses to provide feedback on false positives/negatives, which helped retrain the model.

Over 18 months, triage accuracy improved, and nurses reported higher confidence. Sepsis mortality dropped by 9%. But the real success was in developing a culture where human judgment and machine insight were seen as allies.

Ethical Guardrails: Designing for Equity and Safety

AI doesn't just reflect human bias — it can magnify it. If a predictive model is trained on historical data with embedded disparities, it can perpetuate those patterns.

Healthcare leaders must insist on the following:

- Bias audits during model development
- Demographic-specific accuracy checks

- Patient-centered feedback loops
- Transparent model governance structures

Ethics cannot be outsourced to the data team. It must be led from the top.

Reimagining Leadership Skills in the Age of AI

To lead with AI is to re-skill as a strategic orchestrator. Future leaders must:

- Become fluent in data conversations without being overwhelmed.
- Build cross-disciplinary teams that blend analytics with empathy.
- Navigate gray areas where values and probabilities collide.
- Champion governance that balances innovation and caution.

This is not just technical leadership — it's ethical, adaptive, and visionary leadership.

Conclusion: Intelligence, Reimagined

The organizations that will thrive in healthcare's next era will not be those with the flashiest AI. They will be those with the most profound clarity on how to use it — and the most assertive leadership to guide it.

Human-machine intelligence is not a threat to healthcare leadership. It is the next frontier. And those who embrace it wisely will not only improve care — they will redefine what leadership itself means in the 21st century.

In the next section, we'll explore the ethical implications of this shift — and how to lead with principle in a time of unprecedented technological possibility.

Section 2: Ethical Leadership in an Automated World

THE ETHICAL LEADERSHIP TOOLKIT

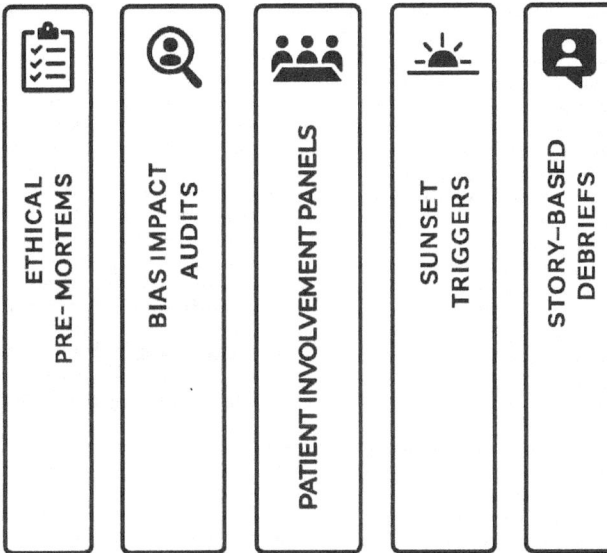

ETHICAL PRE-MORTEMS	BIAS IMPACT AUDITS	PATIENT INVOLVEMENT PANELS	SUNSET TRIGGERS	STORY-BASED DEBRIEFS

As algorithms enter the clinical and administrative space — recommending treatments, prioritizing resources, guiding staffing, and automating workflows — leaders face a new mandate: to act as strategic drivers of innovation and as ethical stewards of its consequences.

This section unpacks what ethical leadership means in the age of automation. It provides a practical, values-centered approach for navigating one of the most complex transformations healthcare has ever faced. Because AI may never replace human leaders — but it will redefine what leadership requires.

The New Moral Terrain of Healthcare Technology

Technology is not neutral. Every algorithm reflects values, assumptions, and priorities — whether conscious or not. In healthcare, where the margin for error is life itself, these embedded choices matter deeply.

Examples of ethical dilemmas introduced by automation include:

- Bias in risk scores that deprioritize certain racial or socio-economic groups for interventions
- Opaque denial algorithms used by payers to automatically reject claims
- Resource allocation models that prioritize efficiency over equity
- Automation of layoffs through productivity surveillance tools
- Data use without patient consent, even for models trained on anonymized data

These are not futuristic hypotheticals — they're already happening. Ethical leadership is no longer a philosophical ideal but a daily operational responsibility.

The Five Ethical Tensions of AI in Healthcare

Leaders navigating automation must grapple with five recurring tensions:

1. Efficiency vs. Equity AI often optimizes for speed, throughput, or cost. But what if the most efficient path isn't the most just one?

2. Prediction vs. Discrimination AI can forecast risks. But if trained on biased data, it may institutionalize past injustices — treating race or zip code as proxies for outcomes.

3. Automation vs. Human Dignity Reducing administrative burden is reasonable. But what if it erodes relational care or replaces critical human judgment with rigid rules?

4. Innovation vs. Accountability: Moving fast can save lives. But who is responsible when an AI-driven decision causes harm?

5. Transparency vs. Complexity AI models, especially deep learning, are often black boxes. But how do we explain decisions we can't fully understand?

Ethical leadership is the art of holding these tensions — not resolving them, but leading through them with clarity and courage.

Building Ethical Infrastructure: More Than Just Compliance

Ethical leadership requires infrastructure. This means going beyond one-off reviews and building systems that embed ethical reflection into the AI design, deployment, and evaluation lifecycle.

Key elements of ethical infrastructure include:

- AI Ethics Committees: Cross-functional groups (clinical, legal, patient, data science) that review models before and after deployment.
- Bias Impact Assessments: Audits that evaluate fairness across race, gender, income, geography, and clinical need.
- Ethical Design Standards: Guidelines that require explainability, reversibility, and patient-centricity.
- Continuous Feedback Channels: These are for users and patients to flag concerns and trigger real-time reviews.
- Governance Scorecards: Dashboards that track performance and ethical health — who benefits, who is harmed, and who is left out.

Ethics as Culture: The Leader's Role

Culture is what people do when no one is watching. Ethical leadership creates cultures where:

- People feel safe speaking up about technology concerns
- Data scientists see themselves as caregivers, not just coders
- Clinicians are not punished for rejecting algorithmic recommendations

- Operations teams know that slowing down for ethics is a form of acceleration
- This culture starts at the top. Leaders must:
- Tell ethical stories, not just success metrics
- Acknowledge uncertainty instead of faking precision
- Normalize disagreement, doubt, and diversity of thought

As one CMO put it: "If we don't make room for ethics in the hallway conversations, we'll never make room for it in the boardroom."

The Ethical Leader's Toolbox

1. Ethical leadership in automation is not abstract. It's a discipline. Here are five practical tools every leader should use:
2. Ethical Pre-Mortems Before launching a new algorithm, gather a diverse team to ask: "If this fails ethically, why will it have failed?"
3. Cross-Check Templates Create a checklist that includes:
   a. Who was consulted?
   b. What data was used?
   c. What are the known limitations?
   d. Who might be disproportionately affected?
4. Patient Involvement Panels Bring patient voices into early-stage development, not just post-rollout PR.

5. Sunset Triggers Define conditions under which an algorithm must be paused or retired, including unintended harm or deteriorating performance.

6. Story Debriefs After implementation, ask frontline teams: "What story is this tool telling? Whose story is missing?"

These tools may not eliminate harm. But they create the moral reflexes that protect against it.

Case Study: Automation Gone Awry in Behavioral Health

A large payer implemented an AI tool to identify high-cost behavioral health patients and recommend tiered interventions. But after six months, clinicians noticed:

- The tool systematically deprioritized patients with bipolar disorder who had irregular service histories.
- Patients with frequent ER visits were flagged, but those who had stopped seeking care (due to stigma or access barriers) were invisible.
- Cultural and linguistic differences weren't accounted for, skewing engagement predictions.

The result: widening disparities.

Leadership responded by:

- Pausing the tool
- Re-training it with community-informed data
- Building a hybrid model with human review of all tier assignments

This wasn't a technical problem. It was a failure of ethical design that required leadership willing to admit that harm had occurred — and change course.

Ethics at the Speed of Innovation

Many leaders fear that ethics will slow innovation. But the opposite is true: ethical clarity accelerates trust, adoption, and impact.

Organizations that integrate ethics into their innovation DNA:

- Launch faster by reducing resistance
- Scale smoother by addressing stakeholder concerns early
- Recover quicker from mistakes because systems for reflection are already in place

As the saying goes: "Fast is smooth when smooth is ethical."

Future-Proofing the Role of Leadership

As automation expands, leaders will be judged not only by what they build — but by what they choose not to.

Ethical leadership will mean:

- Saying no to impressive but harmful algorithms
- Asking inconvenient questions when everyone else is celebrating metrics
- Protecting patient dignity even when the data says otherwise

It will also mean teaching ethics. Embedding it in leadership development. Reward it in performance reviews, and speak publicly about it when others stay silent.

Conclusion: Integrity is the Innovation

In the age of AI, ethical leadership is not a constraint. It is the innovation. It is how healthcare earns the trust to use powerful tools in deeply human domains.

The leaders who will shape the future are not those with the flashiest dashboards. They are the ones who hold complexity with courage, lead with integrity, and design systems where technology serves humanity — not the other way around.

The following section will explore how to address the AI literacy gap — the knowledge divide that limits adoption, trust, and impact. Because if we are to lead in an automated world, we must ensure everyone understands the world we're building.

Section 3: Closing the AI Literacy Gap

As AI and data-driven tools become central to healthcare transformation, a new form of inequality is emerging — the AI literacy gap. This divide isn't about access to care, technology, or infrastructure. It's about understanding. The people responsible for implementing, operating, and benefitting from AI are often ill-equipped to engage with it critically, ethically, or effectively.

This gap shapes decisions, perceptions, and outcomes from boardrooms to break rooms. A brilliant AI solution will fall flat if clinicians don't trust it, patients don't understand it, or administrators can't explain it. But this is not simply a training problem. It is a cultural reckoning, a challenge of organizational readiness, and a test of leadership commitment.

To build a brilliant healthcare system, we must democratize AI knowledge. This isn't about turning everyone into a data scientist — it's about giving everyone the confidence, language, and judgment to navigate a world where machines increasingly shape medical decisions.

Beyond the Buzz: Why AI Literacy Must Be Reframed

Too often, AI literacy is framed narrowly — as a technical upskilling initiative or an IT workshop delivered after implementation. But this misses the more profound truth: AI literacy is about power. It's about who gets to question the tools that shape decisions, who understands their limitations, and who gets left out of the conversation.

In a nurse huddle, AI might be a recommendation engine buried in a triage tool. On the physician dashboard, it's a risk score that subtly changes clinical urgency. To a patient, AI shows up in how long they wait, what options they are offered, or whether a human even enters the room. The literacy gap isn't just knowledge-based. It's lived.

If we want to lead responsibly, we must stop treating AI as a black box to be respected and start treating it as a partner to be understood.

The Landscape of Uneven Understanding

In one organization, a group of administrators began using predictive analytics to forecast staffing needs. When a model predicted reduced surgical demand, shifts were cut. However, clinicians were never told the reasoning behind those decisions. A story of distrust emerged: "They're cutting staff because some robot said so." In reality, the model had simply flagged historical trends. The outcome wasn't unethical — but the communication was.

In another system, a chatbot designed to support mental health triage quietly escalated hundreds of cases to emergency referrals based on a pattern of phrases. The language was benign, but the model had been trained on a narrow linguistic dataset. It confused cultural idioms with clinical red flags. For weeks, nobody questioned the logic.

When the error was found, patients were furious. Their dignity had been reduced to a misunderstood phrase.

These are not edge cases. They are daily reminders of what happens when the people affected by AI are not invited to understand it.

Rethinking Education: From Content to Confidence

AI literacy is not about memorizing definitions. It's about building interpretive capacity. A nurse may never open a Python script, but they must be able to ask: "What variables went into this recommendation? Does it match what I'm seeing at the bedside?" A board member may never design a machine learning model, but they must be able to ask: "What assumptions is this model making about risk, fairness, or cost?"

We must replace traditional instruction with stories, scenarios, and active reflection to get there. Imagine a workshop where a risk algorithm falsely deprioritizes a patient based on zip code. A small group is asked: Would you follow this recommendation? Why or why not? The discussion leads to a deeper insight: the model isn't broken but reflects a world that is.

The heart of literacy is not comprehension but discernment, not instruction but engagement. In many ways, it is not teaching but unlearning — unlearning the notion that the machine must always be correct.

Humanizing AI Through Narrative

Nothing closes a gap faster than a story. At one Midwest health system, AI workshops didn't begin with technical diagrams — they started with a story: a nurse who ignored an algorithmic flag and saved a patient's life. Not because she distrusted technology but because she trusted her intuition. The lesson wasn't to fear AI but to stay human beside it.

Every role has a story. An operations director might recount how an algorithm helped prevent overtime spikes. A data scientist might explain how they learned to build models with real people in the room. A medical assistant might describe how a recommendation felt — helpful, patronizing, neutral. When shared, these stories build collective intelligence — not only about how to use AI but how to live with it.

In a system striving to be wise, stories are the emotional intelligence that prevents arrogance. They remind us that even the most accurate prediction must meet the messy truth of human life.

Walking the Floor: Leadership at the Point of Use

Closing the literacy gap cannot be done from a podium. Leaders must walk the floor. They must stand beside a charge nurse and ask: "Do you know why this flag appears?" They must visit the call center and ask: "How do you feel when the chatbot suggests something before you do?"

They must talk to patients who received automated discharge plans and ask: "Did that feel like care?"

Leadership here is not about answers — it is about presence. It is about building trust not through knowledge alone but through humility.

In one executive rounding session, a team realized the AI-powered length-of-stay model was only visible on a back tab of the EHR, which most residents never checked. The problem wasn't literacy — it was design. But the conversation revealed something else: the people who were supposed to trust the model had never been trained, asked, or engaged. They were not resistant. They were invisible to the process.

A New Literacy Ethos: Engagement as a Two-Way Street

Let us redefine literacy as a system behavior, not a personal deficit. In literate organizations, algorithms are not mysterious edicts handed down from above. They are tools developed in conversation with their users. They are critiqued, refined, and sometimes rejected — not as an act of rebellion but as an act of alignment.

A predictive model was introduced in one pediatric network to flag high-risk asthma patients. Early results were mixed. Then, a team of respiratory therapists sat down with the data science team and redefined the model's thresholds based on what they saw every day in the clinic. Within six months, accuracy improved. More importantly, confidence rose. The model wasn't just innovative, it was theirs.

That's literacy in action. Not perfect understanding, but shared authorship.

The Future We Are Writing

AI literacy will not arrive with a memo. It must be written, practiced, challenged, and lived. The systems that thrive tomorrow will be those that learned to think out loud, to ask questions of their tools, and to build wisdom alongside data.

Because at its core, AI literacy is not just about learning how machines think — it's about remembering how humans do.

In the next section, we will explore how to build governance structures that reflect this spirit — not just technical oversight but shared accountability that keeps the machine in service of care, not control.

Section 4: Operationalizing Trust — Transparent Governance and Shared Accountability

Trust is not an abstract virtue in healthcare — it is the infrastructure on which every system, every interaction, and every outcome depends. And yet, in the age of artificial intelligence and automated decision-making, trust can feel increasingly elusive. As machines begin to guide patient care, allocate resources, and predict risk, the human question remains: Who is accountable?

This section explores what it means to operationalize trust — not as a vague ideal but as a visible architecture of governance, transparency, and shared responsibility. It argues that healthcare leaders must move from managing systems to stewarding trust deliberately, proactively, and visibly in the era of algorithmic influence.

From Assumption to Accountability

Historically, healthcare trust has been assumed. Patients trusted doctors by default. Staff trusted their organizations because the mission was clear. Technology was seen as a tool, not an actor. But AI challenges all of this. Who do we hold responsible when a machine recommends a diagnosis, prioritizes a referral, or denies a claim?

Accountability cannot be left to informal culture in a complex, distributed system. It must be built into how decisions are made, reviewed, communicated, and owned.

At one health system, a surgical risk model erroneously flagged older Black patients as higher risk than their clinical profiles warranted. The team later discovered that the model had been trained on incomplete data — but there was no governance protocol to audit or respond. The issue wasn't malice. It was invisibility.

Invisibility is dangerous. Not because it implies bad intent but because it allows harm to go unchecked. In this context, governance is not bureaucracy — it is moral infrastructure. It ensures that every AI-driven decision has a lineage, a rationale, and, most importantly, a person behind it willing to stand accountable.

The Pillars of Transparent AI Governance

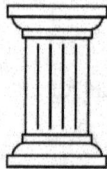

Operationalizing trust requires robust, visible governance. But this governance must go beyond technical validation. It must be ethical, participatory, and anchored in real-world impact. The most effective models share three traits:

The Pillars of Transparent AI Governance

Visibility	Traceability	Accountability
The organization knows what AI models are in use, who owns them, and what they do	There is a clear path from outcome to origin— leaders can trace any output back to its logic, data, and assumptions.	Every model has an identified steward empowered to monitor performance and address unintended harm

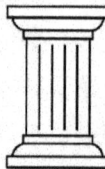

These principles are not theoretical. They must live in org charts, dashboards, workflows, and escalation paths. Every algorithm in use should be traceable, like a clinical order. If a model flags a patient as high-risk, the attending physician should be able to view the logic, see the data points used, and understand the trade-offs made during model training.

The governance process must also be iterative. As clinical pathways are updated with new research, AI tools must evolve with new data, shifting care models, and frontline insights.

Case Study: Rebuilding Trust Through Open AI Committees

After an extensive East Coast academic system experienced backlash over an AI model used in ED triage, leadership created a cross-functional "AI Oversight Committee." Unlike typical quality or compliance teams, this group included frontline nurses, social workers, ethicists, and patient advocates.

The committee had three mandates:

- Review and approve all new AI tools before implementation.
- Audit existing tools for bias, accuracy, and integration fidelity.
- Maintain a public registry of all AI models, their purpose, and performance indicators.

Within a year, staff confidence in AI tools rose by 28%. Perhaps more significantly, clinical complaints about "invisible decision-making" dropped sharply. Governance didn't just improve safety — it rebuilt trust.

What made this committee work was not just its scope but its transparency. Meeting notes were shared system-wide. Tool performance was discussed in open forums. Feedback from clinicians was not only encouraged but tracked. The governance body became a symbol of accessibility and, therefore, trust.

Shared Accountability: Beyond the Data Team

One of the most common failures in AI oversight is the assumption that governance is a "data thing." But proper accountability is distributed. It touches every role:

- Executives ensure alignment with values and strategic priorities.
- Clinicians provide feedback on accuracy, usability, and clinical appropriateness.
- Data scientists explain model design, limitations, and drift.
- Operations leaders monitor workflow impacts.
- Ethicists and compliance officers review fairness and risk.
- Patients share lived experiences with the outcomes AI helped shape.

Accountability works when it is embedded in conversation, not isolation. AI ethics hurdles were introduced in one health system as a monthly practice — informal, cross-functional conversations where staff could raise questions about AI usage. These hurdles often flagged blind spots the technical teams had missed: culturally specific language misclassified by NLP tools, patients misgendered by intake algorithms, or surge planning tools that ignored caregiver burden at home.

Accountability is not a committee. It is a culture.

Leading with Humility: Governance as a Trust Practice

When governance is done poorly, it feels like control. When done well, it feels like stewardship. The difference is humility. Leaders who operationalize trust admit that models are imperfect, that data has gaps, and that human judgment must remain central.

In one California-based health network, an AI tool built to reduce unnecessary imaging began missing early-stage tumors. Rather than hide the failure, the CMO issued a transparent memo to staff and patients, outlined corrective steps, and invited public feedback. The reaction? Trust deepened. Because trust is not built through perfection; it's built through honesty.

Humility also involves acknowledging what we don't know. A forward-thinking CIO once told her staff, "*Every time we use AI to make a decision, we owe someone an explanation — even if we're not fully confident in the model. Because people don't want magic, they want meaning.*"

Designing for Ongoing Learning

Governance cannot be static. AI evolves. So must the structures that manage it. This means:

- Regular model audits and revalidations.
- Escalation paths for frontline concerns.
- Patient feedback loops that inform algorithm adjustments.
- Ongoing staff training about updates and changes.

Some systems now treat AI models like clinicians, requiring credentialing, ongoing education, and annual review. While symbolic, this approach sends a powerful message: AI is not magic. It is a practitioner, subject to scrutiny.

But ongoing learning also applies to leaders. Governance boards must evolve. Training modules must incorporate lessons from past missteps. Transparency reports must be public, not just internal. And most importantly, patient communities must be kept in the loop — not as an afterthought, but as collaborators.

One system even developed "AI Ambassadors" — frontline clinicians trained to explain AI tools to patients and gather real-time feedback. These ambassadors became a bridge, translating data into understanding and turning models into relationships.

A New Ethos of Leadership

At its core, transparent governance is not about technology but identity. What kind of healthcare system do we want to be? Who do we choose to include in decisions? How do we show our values not just in words but in systems?

Operationalizing trust is not a one-time design. It's a leadership practice. It's the repeated, visible, courageous choice to invite scrutiny, share power, and prioritize dignity over speed.

Because in the age of AI, trust is not a passive benefit. It is an intentional outcome that must be architected, protected, and lived.

In the final section of this chapter, we'll explore what it looks like to lead the future — not with fear but with fluency, where vision, data, ethics, and people come together as one voice.

Section 5: Leading the Future — Vision, Fluency, and Human-Centered Strategy

Data and artificial intelligence are redrawing the healthcare landscape. Yet the leaders who will define the future are not the ones who master every algorithm or platform — they are the ones who can translate these tools into systems of healing, trust, and human dignity. In this final section, we explore what it means to lead with authority, fluency, foresight, and integrity.

Fluency is more than technical competence. It is the ability to think, speak, and decide across domains. It is the emotional and ethical intelligence to lead teams through complexity, ambiguity, and innovation. The fluent leader doesn't just understand the power of AI — they understand its context. They know when to accelerate when to pause, and when to step aside so that other voices can shape the conversation.

Vision Rooted in Humanity

True vision is not about predicting which tool will trend next. It's about imagining the kind of healthcare system we want to live in — and then building it with intention. This vision must begin and end with people: patients, providers, and communities.

Consider a children's hospital that embarked on a five-year strategic plan. The first page didn't mention AI, robotics, or blockchain. It asked: "What would it look like if every child felt safe here?" That simple, radical question shaped their decisions — from how they integrated chatbots in mental health triage to how they trained staff in trauma-informed design. AI became one of many instruments, not the melody itself.

Visionary leadership resists the temptation to lead with technology. Instead, it begins with a promise — and then asks what tools will help us keep it.

The **VISIONARY** Leader Model

Nine Traits of Leaders Who Shape the Future

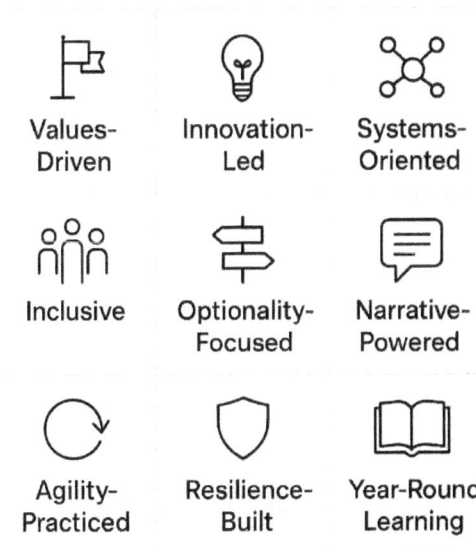

Values-Driven	Innovation-Led	Systems-Oriented
Inclusive	Optionality-Focused	Narrative-Powered
Agility-Practiced	Resilience-Built	Year-Round Learning

Nine Traits of Leaders Who Shape the Future

Case Study: Aurora Pathways Health — A Fluency Reset

Aurora Pathways Health, a five-hospital network in the Pacific Northwest, implemented an AI tool to predict readmission risk. Technically, it worked. Operationally, it backfired. Nurses felt the model overruled their clinical instincts. Patients were flagged for interventions without understanding why. Trust eroded quickly.

Recognizing the issue wasn't just technical, the COO initiated what they called a "Fluency Reset."

They paused new AI deployments and launched a system-wide listening campaign. Interdisciplinary teams — data scientists, social workers, nurses, and ethicists — were together for "AI Reflection Rounds." These weren't audits. They were conversations. The question wasn't, "Did the model work?" It was, "How did it feel?"

The process led to significant changes:

- Risk scores were contextualized with plain language.
- A cross-functional AI Design Council was formed.
- Patient voices were included in the model evaluation.

Six months later, the same tool was reintroduced. This time, the staff used it. Patients trusted it. And leadership didn't just regain credibility — they redefined what it means to govern AI with care.

The SUMIT Leadership Model

To equip healthcare leaders for this new terrain, we introduce the SUMIT model — a five-part leadership philosophy for an AI-shaped world:

The SUMIT Leadership Model

S	**Stewardship of Systems** Leaders act not as technology owners, but as stewards of complex ecosystems—aligning digital strategy with human needs.
U	**Understanding Across Disciplines** Leaders translate data models across clinical, operational, engineering, and ethical boundaries to reduce blind spots.
M	**Moral Courage** Leaders must have the courage to pause implementation if technology compromises care, privacy, or equity.
I	**Innovation with Integrity** Innovation must serve purpose.it listens before solving. It measures what matters, not just what's easy to count.
T	**Transparency in Action** Transparency builds trust—leaders must narrate algorithmic choices and create feedback loops to prevent mistrust.

The SUMIT model is not a template — it's a discipline that centers humanity while embracing transformation.

Building the Capacity for Fluency

Becoming fluent in this new era requires more than a leadership seminar or a webinar on AI trends. It demands a shift in mindset from command and control to co-design. From technology-first to values-first. From implementation speed to psychological safety.

Organizations that prioritize fluency build infrastructure around learning. They establish internal academies for digital literacy. They elevate clinicians into "Digital Translators" who help bridge the IT and care delivery gap. They reward curiosity, not just compliance.

Fluency became required for all senior leaders in one extensive academic system. A monthly forum — called "Data in the Real World" — brought together frontline voices and analytic teams to debrief where models failed and succeeded. The result was not just better tools — it was better trust.

Leading in the Tension Between Scale and Soul

As AI enables scale, the temptation is to treat people like data points. However, leadership requires us to hold the tension between scale and soul. A fluent leader knows how to drive system-wide innovation without losing the intimacy of care.

They ask, before every deployment: Who benefits from this? Who might be harmed? Whose voice is missing? What blind spots are we not yet seeing?

They embed empathy into implementation. They understand that a human brain interprets every dashboard. Every automation displaces a moment of eye contact unless we're intentional.

This is the kind of fluency the future demands: not just knowing what an algorithm predicts — but understanding how it lands in the heart of a nurse, the routine of a family, or the soul of a clinician.

A Leader's Final Frontier

To lead in the next era is to become both architect and anchor — designing systems of intelligence while grounding teams in shared purpose.

The question is not whether AI belongs in healthcare. It already does. The question is whether we are building the leadership capacity to meet this moment.

As we look ahead, let this be the test of leadership: Not how fast we implement, but how wisely we choose. Not how advanced our tools are but how human our systems remain.

Chapter 5: Reimagining Workforce and Organizational Culture

Section 1: Beyond Burnout – Rebuilding Trust, Purpose, and Psychological Safety

Healthcare's most incredible resource is not data, capital, or infrastructure — it's its people. And right now, that resource is strained, frayed, and, in many places, quietly breaking. Burnout, moral injury, and attrition are not just side effects of a stressed system. They are evidence that the human core of healthcare has been misaligned with the structures built around it.

This section is not another call to fix burnout by offering yoga classes, resilience apps, or more productivity dashboards. It is a more profound reckoning: a reimagination of how we lead people, build belonging, and create cultures where healing is possible — not just for patients but for staff, too.

The Limits of Resilience Rhetoric

For too long, we've framed burnout as a personal weakness or a lack of coping skills. We told exhausted nurses to practice mindfulness. We handed overworked physicians toolkits on time management. Instead of questioning why they were in a storm with no life raft, we asked people who were drowning to learn how to swim faster.

Burnout is not a personal deficit. It is a cultural outcome. It tells us how we structure work, measure performance, and value people is fundamentally broken. And no amount of meditation can fix that.

This misconception has fueled an entire industry around individual wellness that, while well-intentioned, often misses the root cause. The message inadvertently becomes: "You're struggling because you're not strong enough." In reality, people are strong. It's the system that has failed them.

To move forward, we must shift from resilience rhetoric to systems repair. That begins with trust.

The Fragility of Trust in a Hyper-Driven System

Healthcare trust is eroding. And not just between patients and providers but within teams, disciplines, and hierarchies. Staff feel surveilled not supported. Clinicians feel micromanaged by metrics. Leaders feel isolated by impossible expectations.

When people lose trust in their organization, everything slows down: decision-making, innovation, and compassion. People become transactional. Fear replaces creativity. Burnout is not just emotional exhaustion — it's the absence of trust.

We must understand how trust is built and how it is broken. It is built in micro-moments: when a leader listens without interrupting, when a policy reflects humanity over expediency, and when feedback is solicited and acted upon. And it is broken just as easily — when transparency is replaced by spin when voices are ignored, when blame becomes the default.

Rebuilding that trust starts by naming the problem. Leaders must say what everyone already knows aloud: "The system is asking too much. And we are going to change that together."

Psychological Safety as a Strategic Imperative

Psychological safety — the belief that one can speak up, ask for help, or make a mistake without punishment — is no longer a luxury. It's the foundation of high-functioning teams, especially in environments shaped by AI, data, and constant change.

In psychologically safe cultures:

- Nurses can challenge algorithmic decisions without fear.

- Residents can admit uncertainty without risking their reputation.
- Executives can ask naive questions without appearing out of touch.
- Staff feel seen, not just tracked.

The presence of psychological safety often determines whether technology becomes an enabler or a threat. In organizations where people are afraid to speak up, flawed algorithms go unchallenged, risks are hidden, and innovations stall. In organizations where safety is prioritized, technology becomes a partner — questioned, refined, and improved.

Creating this kind of safety requires more than good intentions. It demands modeling vulnerability, rewarding dissent, and embedding safety into structures: onboarding, rounds, reviews and debriefs. It means training middle managers in operational processes and relational leadership. It means shifting from a performance-only mindset to one where learning, inquiry, and empathy are core values.

The Power of Shared Purpose

One of the most potent antidotes to burnout is purpose — but only when it's shared, not prescribed. Healthcare workers don't need slogans about the mission. They need leadership that aligns strategy with their daily realities.

Purpose cannot be delivered top-down. It must be co-created. When leaders invite staff to shape vision, redesign workflows, and solve systemic problems together, purpose becomes a living force, not a poster on the wall.

This means:

- Inviting staff to co-design new workflows, not just execute them.
- Linking metrics to meaning — explaining why efficiency matters.
- Making room for joy and recognition in moments of success.

At one safety-net hospital, a CEO began every town hall by inviting a frontline team to share a story of patient impact. Not metrics. Not awards. Stories. It reconnected people to why they entered healthcare in the first place. And over time, those stories became strategy—shaping where the system invested, hired, and innovated.

Listening as an Act of Leadership

Too often, listening is seen as a soft skill. But in today's environment, listening is a leadership competency. It is how we understand what matters, how we surface blind spots, and how we prevent harm.

In one extensive integrated health system, a Chief People Officer instituted a "listening lab" approach — confidential, facilitated monthly discussions with different staff groups. Topics ranged from fear of automation to moral distress in end-of-life decisions. The outcomes were not just cathartic. They shaped executive decisions, policy updates, and organizational design.

Listening builds trust. But more importantly, it builds alignment. People are far more willing to engage with change when they've had a voice in defining the problem.

Belonging Over Perfection

Healthcare has long been shaped by perfectionism — zero harm, flawless execution, and best practices. While quality is non-negotiable, the obsession with perfection can dehumanize those delivering care.

We don't get excellence when staff feel they must permanently hide mistakes, suppress questions, or present a polished front. We get silence.

Belonging requires imperfection. It means creating cultures where people can show up fully — uncertain, grieving, hopeful, and growing, where diversity is not just demographic but experiential, where vulnerability is not a weakness but a credential.

Teams that belong together adapt faster, recover from failure more quickly, and deliver care with more compassion. Belonging is not an HR initiative. It's a survival strategy for the future of work.

A Culture of Renewal, Not Just Retention

Most retention strategies today focus on benefits, bonuses, or schedule flexibility. These matter — but they're not enough. People don't stay for perks; they stay for meaning. For growth. For leaders who see them.

A culture of renewal focuses not just on keeping staff but on restoring them. It makes room for grief. It acknowledges trauma. It creates time and space for reflection — not just productivity.

In one hospital, leadership created "pause rooms" where staff could decompress, reflect, and talk with peer support. Utilization skyrocketed. The message was clear: we see you and we care about how you feel, not just how you perform.

Culture is not what you say — it's what people feel when they walk into a shift.

Designing for Wholeness

Reimagining organizational culture is ultimately about designing for wholeness. For too long, healthcare systems have asked people to leave parts of themselves at the door — their emotions, doubts, and identities.

Wholeness means creating systems where people can bring their whole selves to work, where a Muslim nurse can take a prayer break without judgment. Where a grieving physician is offered support without needing to ask. A single parent's caregiving responsibilities are seen as leadership, not liability.

This is not indulgence. It is infrastructure because people who feel whole bring more energy, insight, and loyalty to their work.

From Crisis Recovery to Cultural Renewal

Rebuilding culture after years of trauma requires more than restoring the old normal. It means designing a new one where emotional health is strategic, leadership is relational, and healing includes the healers.

The burnout crisis is not an HR issue. It is a leadership reckoning. It is a cultural transformation challenge. And it is a moral call to action.

We must stop asking healthcare workers to do more with less — and start asking what they need to thrive. We must stop treating emotional exhaustion as a footnote — and start naming it a systems indicator. We must stop pathologizing burnout — and start organizing around recovery.

In the next section, we'll explore how AI and automation can either deepen disconnection or, when deployed wisely, support human flourishing. But that choice depends on the culture we build today — one rooted in trust, not just transformation.

Section 2: Designing Human-AI Collaboration That Works

Artificial intelligence is not coming for healthcare jobs — it's already here, woven into clinical decision tools, predictive analytics, scheduling systems, and patient engagement platforms. Yet, the real question isn't whether AI belongs in healthcare. It's whether healthcare will be wise and intentional enough to design for collaboration — not a replacement.

At its best, AI in healthcare enhances human capacity. It lightens the administrative load, amplifies early warnings, personalizes communication, and identifies trends no human could parse alone. But without thoughtful integration, AI can also dehumanize care, confuse workflows, and undermine professional autonomy.

Human-AI collaboration must be designed. It is not automatic. And it is not neutral. It is an ethical, relational, and strategic act that begins not with the algorithm but with the people who will use it, interpret it, and live with its consequences.

The Myth of Replacement

Popular narratives — especially in media — often frame AI in adversarial terms. Robots versus doctors. Automation versus empathy. But in reality, the most successful AI applications don't replace clinicians. They reorient tasks, rebalance attention, and allow professionals to spend more time where they are irreplaceable: building trust, explaining nuance and delivering care.

For example, in radiology, AI doesn't replace the radiologist. It prioritizes abnormal scans for review. AI flags risky drug interactions in pharmacy but doesn't override clinical judgment. In behavioral health, natural language processing tools can help identify tone or sentiment shifts in patient messages, alerting therapists — not diagnosing on their behalf.

Designing for collaboration means understanding these nuances. It means asking not, *"What can AI do?"* but *"What should AI do — and how should humans be positioned around it?"*

Co-Designing with the End User in Mind

The failure of many healthcare tech implementations lies not in the code but in the context. Tools are deployed without clinician input. Algorithms are dropped into workflows without understanding how decisions are made. Dashboards are built for executives but ignored by nurses.

- Human-AI collaboration starts with human-centered design:
- Involve frontline staff early in the development process
- Test prototypes in real clinical environments, not simulated ones
- Validate not just accuracy but usability and emotional impact

- Reframe implementation as iteration, not a one-time rollout

A sepsis prediction tool initially caused alarm fatigue at one pediatric hospital because it flagged too many non-critical cases. Nurses began ignoring the alerts. After a redesign process — driven by bedside nurses and data scientists — the tool was adjusted to provide a score and a narrative: "Why this patient? Why now?" Adherence improved. So did the outcomes.

Redefining Roles, Not Reducing Them

AI does change roles. But it doesn't have to erase them. Instead, it can elevate specific responsibilities and reduce cognitive overload.

Consider the case of oncology nurses. With AI-driven platforms tracking vital signs and alerting to symptom progression, nurses found they could spend more time educating families, managing emotional distress, and coordinating interdisciplinary care. Their role shifted — not diminished.

In successful organizations, leaders explicitly reframe this shift:

- They celebrate expanded human roles, not just technical gains
- They train staff on interpretation, not just compliance
- They reward collaboration with machines as a new form of expertise

The goal is not a hybrid workforce of humans and machines. It's a rehumanized one — where machines handle the predictable, and humans lead in the personal, the ethical, and the complex.

The Ethics of Delegation

One of the most under-discussed aspects of human-AI collaboration is this: ***What decisions should never be delegated?*** There are moments in healthcare — end-of-life planning, mental health crises, consent for surgery — where the presence of a human is not optional.

Designing for collaboration means drawing ethical boundaries. It means:

- Prohibiting AI-only recommendations for irreversible decisions
- Ensuring every algorithm has a human in the loop
- Flagging moments when human discretion must override automation

Patients deserve to know when interacting with an AI tool — and when a human will intervene. Transparency is part of safety. But it's also part of trust.

Training for Interpretation, Not Just Operation

As AI becomes more embedded, every clinician — from MA to MD — must learn a new skill: how to interpret machine intelligence. This doesn't mean coding or debugging. It means asking:

- What variables is this model using?
- What patterns is it assuming?

- Does this recommendation align with my clinical intuition?

Training must evolve. Instead of just teaching software clicks, organizations must cultivate curiosity, skepticism, and dialogue. Grand rounds should include AI use cases. Huddles should consist of space for questioning tool accuracy. Chart audits should ask, "Was the tool helpful — or did it distort judgment?"

This interpretive mindset is the new clinical literacy. And it is essential for safety.

Trust Is the True Enabler

Technology doesn't build trust. People do. And in human-AI collaboration, trust is the currency of adoption.

Clinicians must trust that tools were built with care, evaluated for fairness, and responsive to feedback. Patients must trust that automation enhances — not replaces — the human connection. Leaders must trust their teams enough to invite critique, revise strategy, and adapt in real-time.

At one Midwest health system, AI adoption rose dramatically only after the organization published "model fact sheets" — plain-language descriptions of how each tool worked, what data it used, and how to challenge its output. Staff said it made them feel "respected," "empowered," and "in control." That is the foundation of effective collaboration.

The Path Forward: Three Commitments

Human-AI collaboration will not succeed through good tech alone. It will require new leadership habits. Here are three commitments every healthcare organization should make:

- Inclusion Before Implementation
  - o Before launching a tool, ask: Who was involved in designing it? Who will use it daily? Have they shaped its development? Inclusion is not optional — it's foundational.
- Transparency as a Design Principle
  - o Every AI output should be explainable. Staff should understand its limits. Patients should know when they're engaging with automation. Opaque systems erode trust.
- Continuous Listening
  - o Implementation is not an end — it's a beginning. Feedback loops must be constant. Success should be measured by speed and how people feel about using the tool.

Conclusion: Designing a Human Future

The future of healthcare will be intelligent — but whether it is human will depend on how we lead today. Human-AI collaboration is not a technical frontier. It is a moral, relational, and cultural one.

If we get it right, AI will not displace the heart of healthcare. It will protect it. It will lift burdens, clarify complexity, and allow people to show up more fully for each other.

But that future is not guaranteed. It must be designed — with wisdom, humility, and care.

Section 3: Rewriting Leadership Models for the Future Workforce

The traditional healthcare leadership model — command-and-control, productivity-driven, policy-enforcing — is cracking under the pressure of a rapidly transforming world. What worked in an era of stable systems and linear growth is struggling in a world of disruption, unpredictability, and technological acceleration. Nowhere is this more evident than in how we lead our people.

The next generation of workforce leadership demands more than operational expertise. It requires emotional fluency, ethical courage, and narrative clarity. Leaders must not only manage change — they must embody it. And perhaps most importantly, they must become stewards of purpose in an age of digital drift.

From Command to Coaching

In a world of continuous uncertainty, employees don't need more directives — they need more dialogue. The leaders who thrive today are not commanders issuing orders from a distance but coaches who listen, frame challenges, and elevate others. Coaching leadership builds agency, not dependency. It teaches people how to think, not just what to do.

Take the story of Dr. Sharma, a department head at a large urban hospital. Amid a significant staffing shortage, instead of pushing harder for overtime, he restructured his team's daily standups around "compassion circles." Each morning, staff gathered for ten minutes — not to review metrics but to share one thing weighing on them or bringing them joy. What started as awkward silence soon became a source of strength. Errors dropped. Turnover slowed. And a team on the brink of collapse became a team of coaches for one another.

His story reflects a broader shift: from transactional oversight to transformational presence. Coaching leadership doesn't mean being soft. It means being authentic. It means asking, "What do you need to succeed?" as often as "What's your output today?"

Organizations that embed coaching into their leadership fabric see a remarkable change: not just in morale, but in performance. Because when people feel seen, heard, and supported, they bring their whole selves to the work.

Strategic Cost Intelligence Loop
From Cost Cutting to Capacity Return

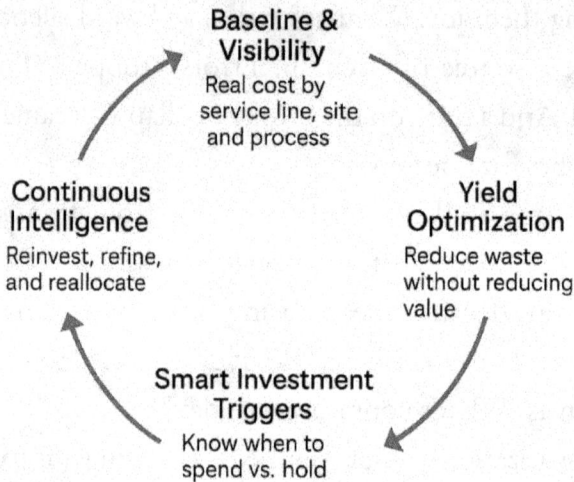

Baseline & Visibility
Real cost by service line, site and process

Yield Optimization
Reduce waste without reducing value

Smart Investment Triggers
Know when to spend vs. hold

Continuous Intelligence
Reinvest, refine, and reallocate

Building Adaptive Capacity

Future-ready leaders are not the most technical — they are the most adaptive. They're the ones who respond to complexity with curiosity, not fear. They view ambiguity not as a threat but as a terrain to navigate.

This demands a shift from fixed identities ("I'm a strategy guy," "I don't do tech") to fluid capabilities ("I'm learning from our nurses on how this impacts care," "I'll shadow the developers before the next meeting").

One health system created a "Leadership Shadowing Rotation," senior executives spent one day a month embedded with a frontline team — from the ED to housekeeping. The goal wasn't observation. It was immersion. Leaders were required to take notes, propose one small process change based on what they saw, and publicly reflect. Over time, staff reported feeling "seen," "valued," and "trusted." Innovation flowed upward, not just downward.

This rotation transformed the C-suite's perspective. One CFO admitted, "I had no idea how much friction our supply systems were causing on night shifts. It changed how I budgeted." Another leader altered the surgical turnaround time policy after witnessing how conflicting documentation practices delayed prep.

Adaptive leaders ask different questions. Instead of, "What's the ROI?" they ask, "What's the unintended consequence?" Instead of "What's the metric?" they ask, "What's the story?"

Storytelling as a Leadership Tool

In moments of change, facts alone don't inspire — stories do. Leaders who can narrate a compelling why, who can connect data to meaning, who can speak with humanity instead of jargon — those are the leaders people will follow.

Consider the story of Maya, a system Chief Human Resource Officer who opened a leadership summit not with a slide deck but with a personal letter from a nurse who nearly quit after a scheduling system failure. Maya read the letter out loud, pausing to acknowledge where the system had failed. Then she pivoted: "This is why we're redesigning, not just rebuilding. Because people like Jasmine deserve more than apologies; they deserve action."

It landed. Not because it was dramatic but because it was real.

Storytelling builds trust. It transforms abstract change into lived experience. And it invites people to become authors of the future, not just actors in someone else's play.

In another case, a CEO facing resistance to automation didn't start by listing efficiency gains. Instead, he shared a story about his father's hospital stay — and how a missed lab alert delayed care. "That's what keeps me up at night," he said. "That's why we're investing in this. To make sure no family has to go through what mine did."

Storytelling is not soft. It is strategic. It builds emotional Alignment before technical implementation.

Distributed Leadership, Not Heroic Leadership

The age of the solo visionary is over. Today's complex problems require collective intelligence. The best leaders create conditions for others to lead — regardless of role, title, or background.

This means:
- Flattening communication layers
- Inviting dissent and debate

- Recognizing leadership behaviors at every level
- Rewarding team success, not just individual brilliance

A quality improvement challenge was launched across departments at a regional medical center. But instead of assigning it to managers, the CMO asked every team to nominate a "micro-leader" — someone who saw problems early and motivated peers to act. The results were profound, not because of budget or software, but because the leadership became localized.

Another example comes from a behavioral health facility where staff were asked to co-create the agenda for town halls. What emerged was not just more engagement but more ownership. Staff brought patient voices, shared innovations, and built peer mentorship models. Leadership became a distributed ecosystem, not a hierarchy.

The Inner Work of Leadership

Leadership in the next era isn't just a role — it's a practice. And it starts within.

Future leaders must invest in self-awareness, emotional regulation, and purpose alignment. This includes:

- Understanding personal biases and blind spots
- Cultivating reflective practices such as journaling, coaching, and feedback
- Developing a leadership identity that evolves with context

One CMO described her growth not through titles but through moments: "When I finally apologized to a nurse publicly when I let a junior analyst run the meeting. When I stopped needing to be the smartest in the room."

Another executive turned her weekly check-ins into reflection sessions. "I stopped asking, 'What did you do?' and started asking, 'What did you learn? What surprised you? What energized you?'" Her team began taking more risks — and owning their growth.

Inner work isn't separate from leadership. It is the bedrock of it. Because how we lead ourselves is how we lead others.

Leading Across Generations

For the first time in modern history, healthcare teams include five generations working side by side. From Silent Generation mentors to Gen Z digital natives, each brings distinct values, communication styles, and leadership expectations.

Leaders must navigate these differences not as challenges but as assets. This means:

- Bridging analog wisdom with digital fluency
- Creating multi-generational mentorship programs
- Designing flexible leadership pathways that adapt to different career arcs

A "reverse mentorship" initiative paired senior surgeons with first-year residents at a teaching hospital to exchange perspectives on AI tools, medical ethics, and lifestyle balance. The result? More empathy, better understanding of burnout across generations, and stronger team cohesion.

Leadership in the future means leading across timelines — honoring the past while making space for what's next.

Conclusion: A New Kind of Leader

The future of healthcare will require leaders who are bilingual in humanity and technology, lead with vision and vulnerability, and hold space for grief and possibility.

The next model of leadership will not be defined by charisma or credentials. It will be determined by impact, presence, and the ability to co-create belonging in constant change.

We are not just rewriting job descriptions. We are rewriting what it means to lead. The transition won't be easy. It will demand courage, reflection, and reinvention. But it will be worth it.

In the next section, we explore how to hardwire these new models into the structure — through hiring, development, evaluation, and succession — ensuring that leadership transformation isn't just aspirational but institutional.

Section 4: Hardwiring Culture Through Structure and Process

Culture does not change because of a keynote speech or a rebranded mission statement. It changes because systems change. For healthcare organizations seeking to build cultures of trust, inclusion, innovation, and resilience, the challenge is not just leadership philosophy — it's operational architecture. Without structural Alignment, even the most inspired cultural goals collapse under the weight of outdated practices.

This section offers a roadmap for turning values into infrastructure. Because in the end, the question isn't what your culture aspires to be — it's what it rewards, what it tolerates, and what it reinforces.

Hiring for Mission, Not Just Metrics

Hiring decisions shape the soul of an organization. And yet, many healthcare systems still rely on transactional hiring practices that reduce candidates' resumes, certifications, and speed of execution. But when you hire someone, you're not just acquiring a skillset — you're inviting a new presence into the cultural DNA of your institution.

At MercySouth, a multi-hospital system in the Southeast, leaders reimagined their hiring philosophy from the ground up. Rather than start tasks must this person perform?" they asked, "What kind of human experience do we want patients and team members to have — and what kind of person will create that?"

They built interview protocols that prioritized storytelling. Candidates were asked to share moments of failure, moments when they advocated for someone vulnerable, and what healthcare meant to them personally. A social worker was hired not because she had the most extended resume but because she shared a story of sitting with a grieving family for hours past her shift. Her presence, it turned out, changed how the team approached end-of-life care.

What you ask in an interview is a mirror of what you value. Hiring becomes culture-building when it prioritizes Alignment, empathy, and mission fit over efficiency and scale.

Onboarding as Cultural Immersion

The first days on the job are a cultural imprint. And yet, in many institutions, onboarding consists of compliance checklists, badging, and rushed introductions. The result? New hires learn systems — but not values. They find out where the break room is but not where the organization's heart lives.

Progressive organizations treat onboarding as narrative-building. At Hopewell Medical, new employees begin with a patient story circle led by long-time staff. They hear real stories — about breakthroughs, ethical dilemmas, and even heartbreaking losses. These aren't sanitized anecdotes. They're the living archive of the culture.

One nurse recounted how, on her first day, she met the maintenance supervisor who told her: "Here, we don't just clean rooms. We reset spaces for healing." That sentence stuck with her more than any policy orientation. It reframed her sense of team.

Effective onboarding doesn't just fill out HR forms — it fills in cultural gaps. It affirms, **"You are part of something meaningful here."**

Performance Reviews That Reflect Values

What you measure reveals what you truly value. Performance evaluations are often misaligned with culture. A health system may value teamwork, but if promotions are based on individual billing or productivity, the cultural message is clear: compete, don't collaborate.

Changing this starts with rewiring evaluation systems. At Radiance Health Network, they shifted from annual reviews to quarterly conversations focused on three pillars: results, relationships, and reflection. Employees were asked:

- What outcomes did you achieve?
- How did you support your team?
- What did you learn or struggle with?

Managers underwent training to provide feedback through the lens of growth, not judgment. They were encouraged to highlight acts of mentorship, emotional labor, and inclusive behaviors.

Over time, the organization noticed a shift. Peer-to-peer recognition increased. Staff began volunteering for cross-department projects. And team morale — once flat — began to recover.

Cultural transformation happens when systems validate what leaders preach.

Embedding Psychological Safety in Process

Psychological safety — the belief that one can speak up without fear of reprisal — is not a mood. It is a system output. It arises not from motivational posters but from deliberate processes that invite voice and normalize vulnerability.

At Ascendant Healthcare, safety rounds were redesigned to include emotional check-ins. Leaders asked staff what they noticed in equipment or protocols and what they noticed in themselves and each other. Initially, many were hesitant. But over time, clinicians shared things like, *"I felt rushed during that code and afraid I'd miss a detail,"* or, *"I wish we had five more minutes to debrief."*

These admissions didn't lead to reprimands — they led to redesigns. More time was added for post-shift reflection. Near-miss reporting increased — not because of more errors, but because people felt safer naming them.

Proper safety is built through rituals that make fear unnecessary.

Leadership Development as Cultural Continuity

Organizations that rise and fall on one charismatic leader are brittle. Durable culture is built through leadership continuity — not just succession, but a pipeline of people who embody shared values.

At Horizon Valley Health, leadership development begins at the unit level. Charge nurses, schedulers, and tech leads are all enrolled in a quarterly workshop called "Voice and Vision." They learn how to mediate conflict, hold difficult conversations, and tell stories that connect people to purpose.

Graduates are mentored by senior leaders and participate in rotational projects across departments. This creates a leadership bench that is broad, diverse, and culturally aligned.

One patient access supervisor who completed the program later shared, "I used to think leadership was about being in charge. Now I know it's about creating clarity and compassion when things get messy."

That's how culture scales — not by cloning a CEO but by cultivating a shared ethos across roles.

Rituals That Reinforce Meaning

Rituals are the heartbeat of culture. They are the repeated, symbolic acts that tell people, "This is who we are." And in healthcare, they matter more than ever —

because this work is emotionally charged, spiritually demanding, and often invisible to the public.

At Loma Central Medical, a simple practice called "Midnight Rounds" transformed the night shift. Once a week, a senior leader would walk the units between 11 PM and 1 AM — not to inspect, but to thank. They brought snacks, asked questions, and occasionally just listened.

For staff who felt forgotten, this became a ritual of inclusion. Nurses began preparing stories to share. Environmental services staff posted anonymous questions on a whiteboard for leaders to answer. The presence of leadership, even for 20 minutes, changed how night staff viewed the organization.

Rituals aren't always grand. But they're always grounded. They are the glue that binds strategy to the soul.

Policies as Moral Documents

Policies are often treated as legal shields — dense, reactive, and written to prevent liability. However, in a values-driven organization, policies can be moral documents. They articulate not just what is permitted but what is protected.

One pediatric health system revisited its policy on social media conduct. Instead of starting with restrictions, it began with trust: "We believe our people are thoughtful, principled, and responsible storytellers. We encourage sharing that reflects our values of dignity and care."

The same was done for the dress code: "Wear what allows you to move freely, think clearly, and confidently serve patients. Let respect, not regulation, guide you."

These words signaled more than rules — they signaled a belief in people. Belief is what policies must be carried out to align with culture.

Conclusion: Building Culture That Lasts

Culture is built where structure meets story. It is reinforced not by posters or slogans but by how people are hired, onboarded, evaluated, developed, and heard. It lives in the systems we create — and the silences we allow.

Culture cannot be left to chance in the quest for high-performing, inclusive, and human-centered healthcare systems. It must be hardwired — not just spoken about in leadership retreats but embedded in hiring rubrics, leadership pipelines, rituals, evaluations, and policies.

However, building culture is not just about Alignment but also about resilience. Every culture will face stressors: leadership transitions, policy shifts, public crises, and even internal moral injury. Organizations that survive these moments aren't the ones with the best slogans. They're the ones whose culture has been stress-tested, whose leaders show up with certainty and care.

This brings us to one of the most overlooked but essential imperatives in cultural change: the workforce's mental health. Systems can only sustain transformation if they actively protect the emotional well-being of their people.

Healthcare workers carry enormous psychological burdens — trauma, decision fatigue, grief, and moral injury. Leaders must treat mental health not as an HR offering but as a foundational strategy. This means designing schedules that allow for rest. It means ensuring access to confidential, non-punitive, and easy-to-navigate counseling. It means integrating trauma-informed leadership into every manager's toolkit.

At BrightPath Health, executives went beyond EAP flyers. They created "reflection rooms" on every floor — quiet, tech-free spaces where staff could decompress. They launched real-time mental health support teams during crisis events. And most importantly, they normalized the conversation. At every all-staff meeting, the CMO began with this line: "You cannot care for others if you run on empty. And you deserve support."

True culture transformation requires this kind of vulnerability from the top. When executives model emotional openness — when they speak of therapy, grief, and burnout — they grant permission for others to be human, too.

So, as you build systems and structures, don't forget the soul. Hardwire your values, yes. But also create space for reflection, renewal, and repair. Remember that culture doesn't live in your dashboards — it lives in your people.

And those people need to know that they matter, not just for what they produce, but for who they are.

In the final section of this chapter, we'll explore how to sustain this transformation over time — ensuring that culture remains a durable, evolving force, even as organizations grow and adapt to new challenges.

Section 5: Sustaining Workforce Transformation in a Changing World

Change is easy to announce, challenging to implement, and nearly impossible to sustain—unless the culture, infrastructure, and leadership remain committed long after the ribbon is cut. Most workforce transformation efforts fade not because of lousy strategy but because of inattention. Momentum dissolves when leaders turn their eyes elsewhere, when urgent crises replace long-term investment, and when wins are celebrated as conclusions rather than beginnings.

In this final section of Chapter 5, we explore how to ensure that the transformation of workforce culture endures. This means building adaptive systems, evolving leadership mindsets, and continuously centering the lived experience of the people who make healing possible daily

Make Culture a Standing Agenda Item

Too often, leaders talk about culture during retreats or when launching a new initiative, however, in organizations where transformation sticks, culture becomes a constant conversation.

At Pacifica Health, every executive team meeting begins with a culture dashboard. Metrics include psychological safety scores, burnout rates, interdepartmental trust ratings, and qualitative anonymous survey quotes. Leaders take turns sharing a "culture moment"—something they saw, heard, or experienced that week reflecting (or conflicting with) core values. This isn't fluff. It's the organization holding a mirror to itself.

By keeping culture front and center, Pacifica could course-correct quickly when remote staff began reporting feelings of isolation. They added hybrid team rituals, virtual mentorship sessions, and monthly "shadowing swaps" across departments. Retention improved, but more importantly, engagement became active, not assumed.

Sustaining change means weaving culture into daily decision-making—not revisiting it only when morale dips or headlines hit.

Design for Renewal, Not Just Resilience

Resilience has become the buzzword of the healthcare workforce. But what if our aim isn't to teach people to endure—but to ensure they can renew?

Organizations that sustain transformation prioritize recovery as much as performance. They understand that energy, creativity, and compassion are finite resources that must be replenished.

Consider the Recovery Rotation at Glenstone Medical Center. Every employee, from porters to physicians, is guaranteed one "recovery week" every quarter. They can use it for professional development, cross-functional learning, or decompression. It's not PTO—it's paid time to reset and reflect.

The result? Fewer sick days. Greater cross-department collaboration. And a culture that signals, "We care about your energy, not just your effort."

Transformations don't last when the people driving them are depleted. Designing for renewal sustains both people and momentum.

Treat Feedback as Fuel

Feedback is not a box to check. It's the engine of cultural evolution. However, to harness it, organizations must create systems that invite, value and act on feedback in real-time.

Starlight Health built a "Feedback-to-Action Lab," a cross-functional team that turned staff insights into rapid experiments. One idea—creating a five-minute "voice check" at the end of shifts—led to a dramatic rise in team connection scores.

When people see their input leads to visible change, they don't just speak up more—they invest more. They shift from being subjects of culture to stewards of it.

Evolve Rituals With Intention

Rituals are powerful, but those meanings can become stale. Sustainable cultures revisit and revise rituals as the workforce evolves.

During the pandemic, Riverside Health's gratitude wall went virtual—an internal platform where staff could tag colleagues with stories of care. When staff returned to the site, they launched "live gratitude" rounds instead of reverting to paper. Leaders walked the floor, reading aloud recent submissions and inviting spontaneous appreciation.

This wasn't nostalgia—it was evolution. Rituals that sustain transformation adapt to the people they serve.

Anchor Culture in Story and Strategy

At the heart of sustainable workforce transformation lies one powerful question: What story are we telling ourselves about who we are becoming?

Narratives drive behavior. When leaders articulate a straightforward, emotionally resonant narrative that links the past to the future and the individual to the collective, culture becomes a living force. It reminds staff that they are not just showing up for a job but contributing to a greater arc of meaning.

At HavenCare, the executive team shared a quarterly "Culture Chronicle," a storytelling bulletin that blended metrics with moments. One edition featured a frontline respiratory therapist who advocated for language-access signage and saw it implemented. Another highlighted a finance manager who rewrote the vendor policy to be more inclusive of local businesses.

But it didn't stop at storytelling. The Culture Chronicle ended with a prompt: "What story do you want to help us write next?" Staff responded with hundreds of ideas—from mental health destigmatization campaigns to trauma-informed care protocols. Culture became a participatory narrative.

Embedding story into strategy transforms employee engagement from passive compliance to personal ownership. Employees become aligned and engaged when they see their values reflected in the organizational narrative.

Transformation won't be sustained through policies alone in today's healthcare workforce. It will be sustained through stories of impact, purpose, resilience, and imagination. When stories and strategy are intertwined, the organization becomes more than a place of employment. It becomes a community of shared identity and evolving possibility.

Conclusion: The Long Game of Culture

Workforce transformation is not a project. It is a way of leading, a way of designing, a way of listening—and a way of living. It is a long game that requires depth, consistency, and patience.

To sustain it, leaders must resist the temptation of closure. There is no finish line in culture—only evolution.

They must listen when the metrics dip and lean in when feedback stings. They must protect time for healing as fiercely as they do for revenue. And they must remember that the most potent signal of an organization's values isn't what it says but what it repeats.

The future of workforce transformation depends on our willingness to slow down and care for patients and those who see them. This means integrating mental health as an operational pillar. It means elevating well-being as a leadership competency. It means recognizing that behind every metric is a human navigating complexity, stress, and emotional labor.

Sustaining culture means designing with humanity in mind. It's about providing scaffolding—not just in structure but spirit. Leaders who show up with humility, who embrace storytelling as a strategy, and who celebrate progress instead of perfection will be the ones who guide their organizations through uncertainty and into a future defined by dignity.

In the healthcare systems of tomorrow, the most admired cultures won't be the loudest—they'll be the most coherent, compassionate, and courageous. They'll be the ones where transformation isn't survived but sustained.

And those will be the systems where patients aren't just treated, they are healed.

Chapter 6: Scaling Innovation Without Losing Soul

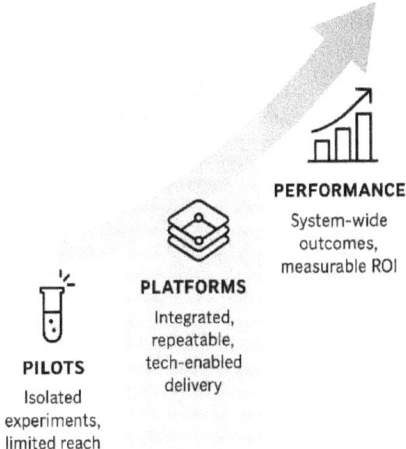

SCALING INNOVATION:
FROM PILOTS TO PLATFORMS
TO PERFORMANCE

PERFORMANCE
System-wide outcomes, measurable ROI

PLATFORMS
Integrated, repeatable, tech-enabled delivery

PILOTS
Isolated experiments, limited reach

Section 1: From Pilot to System-Wide Practice

In healthcare, there's a pattern as predictable as it is frustrating: a promising pilot launches, wins early praise, generates modest success—and then fades into the background. It's not that the idea lacked merit. It's that the system lacked a mechanism to scale it. Between isolated innovation and systemic transformation lies a chasm that too few organizations cross.

This section is about that crossing. It explores how leaders move from experimentation to integration, from lighthouse projects to enterprise strategy, without losing the very soul that made the original idea effective in the first place.

Agile Governance System Map
Redesigning Decision-Making for Transformation Speed

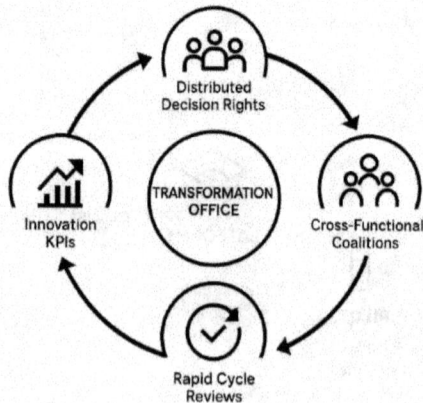

The Pilot Graveyard Problem

Pilots are safe. They're contained. They let organizations explore new territory without disrupting core operations. However, the very thing that makes pilots manageable is also what makes them unsustainable.

Healthcare systems are littered with the remnants of pilots: digital tools that never made it past one department, workflow changes that evaporated after a champion left, and brilliant ideas that died in the handoff to operations.

The problem isn't innovation fatigue—it's integration failure. Leaders often underestimate the cultural, operational, and infrastructural lift required to embed something new into the life of a system. A successful pilot may prove that something can work—but scaling asks whether it will still work under pressure, at volume, across contexts.

Scaling Begins with Design

The secret to successful scaling isn't replication—it's adaptation. Leaders must stop asking, "How do we copy this?" and start asking, "How do we design for scale from day one?"

This means building pilots with portability in mind. It means:

- Including operations and IT from the beginning, not just innovation teams.

- Testing in diverse settings—not just high-performing units.
- Documenting workflows, outcomes, and friction points rigorously.
- Building measurement systems that work in real time, not just retrospectively.

At Evergreen Health, a virtual behavioral health triage model was piloted in a single emergency department. Instead of treating it as a tech deployment, leaders treated it as a system simulation. They included frontline nurses, schedulers, IT, billing, and legal. Within six months, the model spread to six sites—with minor adjustments, not reinvention. Why? The scale was used in DNA from day one.

Champions Make It Real, But Systems Make It Last

Every successful pilot has a champion: the energetic nurse manager, the passionate medical director, and the relentless analyst who keeps pushing. But champions can't be the strategy. Because champions burn out, get promoted, or leave.

If your innovation relies on one person, it's not scalable. Period.

Systems must create institutional muscle memory. This means:

- Building training modules into standard onboarding.

- Embedding responsibilities into roles, not personalities.
- Creating escalation and support pathways that don't rely on one expert.

A new discharge planning tool at a large academic center reduced readmissions in one unit. The pilot champion trained every nurse personally. However, when she transferred, usage dropped by 70%. It wasn't until the tool became part of orientation, with system-wide help desk support, that it became permanent.

Sustainable scaling requires infrastructure—not just inspiration.

Translate Evidence into a Narrative

Data is essential, but it's not persuasive alone. To scale innovation, you need a story that resonates across roles and geographies. Leaders must learn to translate pilot evidence into narrative urgency.

One CMO described a strategy that turned the tide: "We didn't just say the new workflow reduced ED boarding by 20%. We told the story of Mr. Davis—an elderly patient who finally got home before midnight because of our changes. That story made people want to try. The data told them they could."

The narrative becomes the bridge between evidence and action. It answers the unspoken question: "***Why should I care?***"

Identify Scale Accelerators and Friction Points

Scaling doesn't happen in a vacuum. Incentives, politics, workflows, and bandwidth shape it. Leaders must conduct a scale-readiness scan:

- Who will resist this, and why?
- What existing systems support or sabotage it?
- How does this fit into current performance metrics?

At one regional system, an AI-driven staffing tool struggled to expand beyond its pilot unit. Not because the model failed—but because nurse managers in other departments weren't bonused on staffing efficiency. When incentives were aligned, adoption surged.

Scaling isn't just about proving value. It's about designing alignment.

Preserve Soul While Expanding Reach

Perhaps the most challenging part of scaling is not technical—it's emotional. Pilots often feel intimate, mission-driven, and grounded in relationships. As they grow, they risk becoming bureaucratized, abstract, and transactional.

To avoid this, leaders must preserve the human element. This means:

- Keeping end-user voice in continuous improvement loops.
- Creating spaces for feedback, adaptation, and co-ownership.

- Celebrating not just spreads but also local creativity within the model.

At MercyLine, a nurse-led fall reduction initiative spread across 12 hospitals. But each site personalized it: some with visual cues, others with family engagement protocols. Leaders didn't enforce sameness—they enabled resonance.

The soul of innovation isn't in the template. It's in the trust, the care, and the belief that we can build something better—together.

Closing Reflection

Scaling innovation is not a handoff—it's a translation. It's a series of conversations, adaptations, and reinforcements. The leaders who do it best don't just ask, "How do we roll this out?" They ask, "How do we keep this alive?"

In the end, system-wide transformation doesn't start with scale.

It starts with the soul—and then finds a way to grow.

And that soul must be nurtured intentionally. Leaders must remain close to the frontline experiences that inspired the original innovation while elevating those voices into system-level design. They must preserve the why as much as the how reminding teams that scale is not about making everything the same—it's about making everything meaningful.

Sustainable scaling asks us to embrace paradox: to expand reach without diluting impact, to standardize infrastructure while personalizing delivery, and to lead boldly while listening constantly. It requires us to become stewards of culture, not just custodians of process.

Ultimately, scaling healthcare innovation is not just a question of feasibility or ROI. It's a question of identity. What kind of organization do we want to become? What stories do we want our teams to tell five years from now—not about technology or metrics, but purpose?

When we scale with soul, we don't just replicate models—we replicate meaning. We don't just reach more patients—we deepen care. And we don't just build systems—we build belief.

That is the *accurate measure of transformation.*

Section 2: Maintaining Local Wisdom While Growing

In the pursuit of system-wide scale, there's a risk few leaders speak about—but many have felt: the erosion of local brilliance. That intangible wisdom built on the nuances of a community, the culture of a unit, or the improvisation of a high-functioning team often gets lost when scale imposes sameness.

Innovation begins with people. And when we forget that, scale becomes a blunt instrument.

This section explores how to grow innovation without flattening it—how to maintain the richness of local context while ensuring strategic coherence. It's a leadership paradox: build standard frameworks while letting the texture of each site, team, and patient population reshape those frameworks for relevance.

The Risk of Uniformity

Too often, systems define scale as replication. A model works in Hospital A, so we copy it verbatim in Hospitals B through Z. But in doing so, we erase the subtle adaptations that made it work in the first place: the informal communication loops, the specific leadership tone, and the neighborhood-specific patient education tweaks.

Uniformity is efficient—but it's also brittle. It ignores what matters most in healthcare: trust, relationships, and culture. These don't copy well. They have to be co-created.

At CareBridge Health, a care coordination tool was launched in a high-density urban campus with impressive results. But when leadership imposed the exact rollout plan on a rural affiliate, adoption floundered. Why? The local team had fewer social workers, different transportation barriers, and no broadband access in key areas. The failure wasn't in the tool but in the assumption of sameness.

Local Wisdom as a Strategic Asset

The most effective leaders treat local insight not as noise but as a signal. They build models that can absorb variation—not reject it.

At Riverbend Medical, leadership hosted co-design labs at each site when scaling a successful bedside medication verification protocol. Nurses were asked: "How would this fit in your flow? What would get in the way? What would make it easier for your team?" The result wasn't chaos. It was cohesion. Each unit owned its rollout version, but core safety principles remained intact.

Local wisdom often appears in workarounds, informal rituals, and patient-facing communication styles. Instead of eliminating these, scaling leaders seek to understand and elevate them. When you honor the local voice, adoption becomes ownership.

Codifying Flexibility, Not Just Structure

Scalable innovation doesn't mean identical implementation. It means consistent outcomes through locally adapted methods. The key is building a structure that invites discretion—not suppressing it.

This can be done through "guardrails with guidance:"

- Core Requirements: Non-negotiables (e.g., safety checks, data capture standards)
- Recommended Tools: Templates or workflows that can be tailored
- Freedom Zones: Where local teams innovate within a defined scope

For example, in rolling out a digital social determinant of health (SDoH) screening tool across 22 clinics, Apex Health created three required questions, five optional modules, and a space for clinics to add custom screening fields based on their communities. The result? 87% adoption in six months—with clinics reporting more substantial community alignment.

Listening Infrastructure: More Than Surveys

To preserve local wisdom, you must hear it in real-time, just in retrospective surveys. This means building two-way feedback loops into operations:

- Monthly frontline huddles with innovation feedback time
- Embedded "culture translators" or champions who surface local insights
- Micro-grants or time budgets for teams to test local improvements

At Sunfield Behavioral, a "Friday Five" ritual was created: five minutes at the end of each week where staff could write down one thing that worked, one that didn't, and one small idea to try next week. The best ideas were spotlighted system-wide every month. This wasn't performative listening. It was a listening engine that fueled action.

Conclusion: Scaling With Respect

Scaling innovation while preserving local wisdom is not about compromise. It's about creativity. It requires leaders to see variation not as resistance but as relevance. It requires humility—the understanding that those closest to the work often hold the answers we need most.

In systems that grow well, scale is not a force that erases culture. It's a platform that amplifies it.

Everyone in the community is different in terms of healthcare. Every story is specific. And every act of care is local—even when the vision is global.

To get this right, leaders must foster an environment where local intelligence is routinely harvested and celebrated. This means treating pilots and local experiments as R&D laboratories—not outliers to be tamed but assets to be studied and adapted. Leaders must create formal mechanisms to honor informal insights and decision-making processes that reward nuance over uniformity.

It also means embracing a new leadership stance that replaces command-and-control with convene-and-curate. Instead of deploying a solution from the top, leaders gather insights from across the system, find patterns, and shape infrastructure that supports flexibility without sacrificing coherence.

When scaling is done with respect, what emerges is not chaos but resonance. Patients receive care that reflects their realities. Staff feel seen and empowered, not policed. And systems become more agile—not by becoming looser, but by becoming more deeply connected to the wisdom already alive within them.

The sustainable scale doesn't silence local brilliance. It listens to it, protects it, and invites it into the architecture of the future.

And that keeps innovation alive, human, and worthy of being spread.

Section 3: Guardrails for Ethical Expansion

Innovation isn't neutral. Every decision to scale a new model, technology, or process has moral weight—because it affects how care is delivered, who benefits, and who may be left behind. As organizations scale, the pressure to streamline and standardize can often obscure the more profound question: *Are we scaling responsibly?*

Ethical expansion means more than compliance. It requires designing with dignity, transparency, and inclusion at the core. It demands that we don't just ask, "Can we do this everywhere?" but instead, "Should we— and if so, how do we do it in a way that strengthens trust rather than eroding it?"

This section explores the vital guardrails that help leaders expand innovation with impact and integrity.

Principle 1: No Scale Without Equity

It isn't genuinely scalable if a solution only works for the well-resourced or digitally fluent. It's stratified. Equity must be a starting point, not a retrofit.

At Kindred Regional, a virtual triage program was launched with promising early results—reduced wait times and faster follow-ups. However, a closer look revealed that English-speaking, privately insured patients benefited disproportionately. Low-income and limited-English patients were often unable to navigate the system.

The response? The organization paused expansion. They co-designed new access points with community health workers, added multilingual digital navigators, and rewrote protocols to center accessibility.

Ethical scale means checking who's missing from your success metrics—and pulling them in by design, not exception.

Principle 2: Protect the Human Core

As scale introduces automation, protocolization, and digital workflows, the risk is clear: efficiency becomes a proxy for compassion. When we remove friction, we may also remove touch.

Leaders must ask: ***Where does this system allow space for empathy?***

Consider CareFirst's AI-driven diagnostic assistant. It performed well in pilot sites, reducing diagnostic errors and clinician time. However, during expansion, they hardwired one requirement: every AI-suggested plan had to be reviewed with the patient in a shared decision-making session. This preserved the clinician-patient connection while benefiting from technological augmentation.

In ethical scaling, the human relationship isn't a casualty—it's a cornerstone.

Principle 3: Transparency Over Performance Theater

Many systems rush to declare success to justify expansion. But in doing so, they can inadvertently suppress dissent, flatten nuance, or cherry-pick results.

Ethical scale requires transparency about what's working—and what isn't. This includes:

- Publishing not just aggregate outcomes but disaggregated data by population
- Including frontline feedback in scale reports
- Creating safe forums for staff to voice concerns without fear

At UnityHealth, every scaled initiative has a public "Learning Dashboard" where early results, implementation barriers, and lessons learned are shared openly. This not only builds internal trust but also invites improvement in the field.

Ethical expansion embraces imperfection as part of the process, not a threat.

Principle 4: Align Expansion with Mission, Not Just Margin

It's easy for innovations that save time or money to win fast-track approval. However, ethical leadership demands Alignment with a deeper purpose.

One national system declined to scale a cost-saving pharmacy chatbot when patients reported feeling dismissed or confused. Instead, they invested in a hybrid model: automated refills with human pharmacists proactively reaching high-risk patients.

Financial efficiency without mission alignment isn't innovation. It's erosion.

Principle 5: Invite Moral Imagination

Ethical scaling is not about applying rules. It's about cultivating questions. What would it mean to expand this model in a way that heals trust, builds access, and honors complexity?

Create ethical design checkpoints:

- Before launch: Who might be harmed or excluded?
- During scale: What unintended effects are emerging?
- After rollout: Are we still living our values?

At BrightOak Children's, every innovation undergoes a "compassion audit." Patients, families, and frontline staff are invited to assess how the change feels—not just how it functions. It's not perfect. But it signals something powerful: we care not just what works—but what's right.

Conclusion: Scaling With Conscience

The actual test of a health system's values is not what it pilots—it's what it chooses to spread.

Ethical expansion is not about being slow. It's about being deliberate. It's not about rejecting innovation. It's about integrating it with awareness and accountability. And it's not about avoiding risk—it's about accepting responsibility for how we shape the future.

Because when we scale without soul, we might succeed in metrics—and fail in meaning.

But when we scale with conscience, we don't just change systems.

We elevate care.

And more than that—we preserve trust.

Trust is the currency of healthcare. It binds patients to providers, staff to leadership, and communities to institutions. Scaling with a conscience means ensuring that every expansion decision, every workflow redesign, and every digital deployment reinforces that trust rather than weakening it.

In practice, this calls for deeper cross-functional collaboration. Compliance officers must talk with clinicians. Digital architects must listen to patient advocates. Executives must walk the halls—not just the dashboards—to see how change lives in reality, not just in planning decks.

It also calls for courage. Ethical scaling requires us to slow down when we feel the pressure to move fast, ask more challenging questions when it's easier to look away and center the marginalized's experience when success metrics favor the majority.

Ultimately, scaling with a conscience is about legacy. What kind of organization will we leave behind? What will people remember about how we led through transformation?

Let it be this: that we scaled wisely. That we scaled justly. That we scaled with care.

And in doing so, we didn't just expand access.

We expanded humanity.

Section 4: Balancing Standardization and Innovation

In the evolution of healthcare, there is a tension that never quite resolves—nor should it. Standardization offers stability, consistency, and safety. Innovation delivers agility, creativity, and progress. But when pursued in isolation, each becomes brittle. True transformation happens not by choosing one over the other but by leading with the wisdom to balance both.

This is not a middle ground. It is a higher order of leadership—a skill set that belongs at the CEO table, not just in operational teams. The most successful healthcare systems of the future will be those that hardwire Standardization where it counts and unlock innovation where it thrives. They won't ask, "Should we optimize or experiment?" They'll ask, "*How do we build a system where both coexist—by design?*"

When Standardization Goes Too Far

Standardization is essential to scale. It creates a common language across departments, improves safety, and reduces cost. However, Standardization without context becomes a blunt force.

Consider the story of a multi-hospital system that standardized discharge protocols across all facilities. This was a win on paper: efficiency increased, and documentation errors dropped. But in reality, many clinicians reported a growing sense of disconnection from their patients. Nurses could no longer tailor discharge conversations to cultural nuances. One nurse said, *"We followed the script but lost the relationship."*

What began as a quality initiative morphed into something robotic. Staff burnout rose. Patients are left confused. The system had optimized the process—but at the cost of personalization and trust.

When Innovation Becomes Fragmentation

On the other hand, when every department innovates in isolation, systems become noisy. Great ideas emerge—but rarely scale. Worse, they often compete.

A large regional system once celebrated its culture of "permissionless innovation." However, after three years, it found 17 different intake workflows across nine facilities. Patients filled out the same forms multiple times. Data wasn't integrated. The patient's experience fractured.

The problem wasn't creativity. It was the absence of connective tissue—an intentional framework that transformed innovation into shared progress.

Strategic Leadership: Guardrails That Empower

The question isn't whether to standardize or innovate. It's how to create guardrails that ensure freedom within form.

Forward-thinking systems embed innovation pathways that respect enterprise architecture and strategy. One East Coast system launched a "Transformation Council"—a cross-functional body that reviewed local innovations not to control them but to elevate them. They asked three questions:

- Does this align with our mission?
- Can it scale with integrity?
- What can others learn from it?

This wasn't bureaucracy. It was orchestration. Departments felt heard, supported, and connected. Some ideas stayed local. Others became systemwide solutions.

Architecting for Flexibility and Fidelity

Modern healthcare systems must be built like smart cities, with consistent infrastructure and localized expression. This includes:

- Platform-thinking: standardized digital foundations that allow customized front-end experiences.
- Federated governance: clear decision rights that empower local units within strategic boundaries.
- Agile budgeting: flexibility to test and scale ideas without needing yearlong approval cycles.

At Medisphere Health, executive leadership introduced "**adaptive blueprints**"—models that included non-negotiables like safety protocols but left space for site-specific implementation. The result? Faster adoption and deeper ownership.

Culture Is the Operating System

Balancing standardization and innovation is not just a process challenge—it's a cultural one. It's not about the frameworks you build. It's about the mindsets you nurture. Culture is the silent force determining whether innovation is invited or discouraged, whether standardization is embraced or resented.

In high-functioning systems, culture serves as the invisible operating system. It's the difference between employees asking, "Can I try this?" and saying, "Of course I will—this is how we grow." Culture guides behavior in the gray areas where policy is silent, and leadership is distant. It determines whether a nurse feels empowered to adjust a care pathway or a frontline team feels confident enough to challenge a dated workflow.

At Clarion Health, quarterly "Strategy and Story" town halls allow local teams to share innovations, lessons, and failures directly with executives. These aren't superficial showcases. They are cultural rituals reinforcing clarity of purpose and the shared belief that creativity isn't a luxury but a leadership expectation.

One year, a respiratory therapist stood up and shared a process tweak that reduced unnecessary imaging in the ICU. It was a small change but triggered a ripple effect across departments. What followed wasn't a policy memo—it was an email from the CEO highlighting the story and reminding everyone, *"Standardization protects. Innovation elevates. Culture enables both."*

Culture, in this sense, is not the mood of an organization. It is its muscle memory. It teaches teams to move through complexity, respond to ambiguity, and lead from any seat.

Visionary leaders treat culture like infrastructure—not a passive background but an active force to be designed, reinforced, and evolved.

Because, in the long run, it's not the procedures that sustain transformation.

It's the people who believe they have permission to lead it.

Introducing the CORE Culture Model™ – The New Operating System for Transformation

The CORE Culture Model™

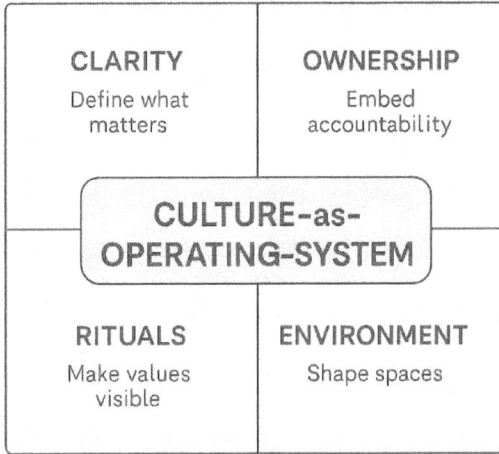

CLARITY Define what matters	OWNERSHIP Embed accountability
CULTURE-as-OPERATING-SYSTEM	
RITUALS Make values visible	ENVIRONMENT Shape spaces

To operationalize culture in an actionable, repeatable, and scalable way across industries, I propose a new universal framework: the **CORE Culture Model™**. CORE stands for Clarity, Ownership, Rituals, and Environment—the four essential pillars that shape and sustain a high-performance, high-integrity culture. This model is designed not as a soft HR initiative but as a strategic operating system that informs decision-making at every level of an organization.

C — Clarity

Without clarity, culture becomes guesswork. Visionary organizations articulate what they do and why it matters—over and over again. Every employee should be able to answer: What do we stand for? What do we expect from each other? What future are we building together? Clarity sharpens Alignment. It eliminates noise. It becomes the foundation of trust.

O — Ownership

Culture doesn't live in mission statements—it lives in behavior. Ownership means every individual feels personally accountable for upholding and evolving the culture. It's the difference between someone waiting for permission and someone taking initiative. Ownership is what transforms values from wall art into daily action.

R — Rituals

Rituals are the heartbeat of culture. They make values visible. They can be as simple as story-sharing at shift change or as structured as innovation town halls. Rituals create emotional glue. They move culture from abstraction to experience. And when done consistently, they become the rituals of belonging.

E — Environment

The environment is where culture lives. This includes not just physical spaces but psychological and digital environments. Are voices heard? Are tools aligned with values? Is there room for pause, reflection, and regeneration? The right climate reinforces the behaviors and beliefs a culture wants to sustain.

Together, these four elements create a system—not a slogan. They form the invisible architecture of organizations' thinking, acting, and evolving. When applied intentionally, the CORE Culture Model™ allows leaders to scale transformation without eroding meaning.

Because in every system, culture is either by design or by default.

The CORE Culture Model™ ensures it's by design.

Conclusion: Leading the Paradox

The great healthcare leaders of tomorrow won't be those who simply demand scale or praise experimentation. They will be those who can live in the creative tension between the two—who see Standardization not as a constraint but as a catalyst for better innovation.

This balance isn't found in a playbook. It's cultivated over time—through governance, infrastructure, and culture that respects precision and possibility.

Because we're not just building healthcare systems that function.

We're building ones that adapt, evolve, and never forget the human beings they were meant to serve.

In the hands of visionary leaders,
Standardization and innovation don't compete.
They compose.

Section 5: The Soul of Scale — Staying Human as You Grow

Growth is a seductive force. It promises impact, reach, and relevance. But in healthcare, the scale can be a double-edged sword. For every initiative that spreads effectively, many lose the very spirit that made them worth scaling in the first place. Efficiency replaces empathy. Uniformity eclipses uniqueness. Mission gives way to machinery.

This section explores how leaders can grow systems without losing what matters most: humanity. It challenges us to redefine scale—not as an expansion of processes but as a deepening of purpose. It also introduces new science-backed, experience-driven methods for embedding empathy, trust, and meaning into growth.

From Scaling Output to Scaling Meaning

Most organizations scale by asking: What worked here? How can we replicate it elsewhere? They focus on outputs—on processes, protocols, and templates. However, what made the original initiative effective was rarely just the process. It was the purpose. The shared belief, the spark of ownership, and moments of human impact made people care.

That's why scaling output without meaning often fails. You end up duplicating tasks without duplicating commitment. You spread the structure but not the spirit.

Visionary organizations ask a different question: What made this work matter—and how do we scale that? They seek to preserve the actions and the emotional architecture beneath them.

Take the example of Mayo Clinic's model of integrated care. Yes, they replicate clinical protocols. But more importantly, they scale behaviors. Every clinician is trained to collaborate across disciplines, to put patient needs above specialty silos, and to carry the same tone of respect and humility. This is not just a transfer of operations—it's a transfer of ethos.

At a systems level, this requires new tools: onboarding rituals that immerse people in the "why," leadership narratives that reiterate the founding story, and design templates that leave room for local adaptation without losing sight of the core mission.

To scale meaning is to treat culture as an asset, not a byproduct. It's to build a future where actions are repeated, and intentions are remembered.

Leaders must make a fundamental shift: stop scaling what was done and start scaling why it mattered.

The most potent innovations don't spread because they are efficient.

They spread because they are alive.

And our job as leaders is to keep that pulse beating— wherever growth takes us.

Embed Narrative Intelligence into Expansion

Humans remember stories, not spreadsheets. If you want your scaled innovation to live, pair it with a narrative that inspires—and, more importantly, one that can travel. The narrative becomes the emotional infrastructure of any transformation. Without it, even the most well-resourced rollouts stall. With it, even modest ideas gain momentum.

Every large-scale rollout should be anchored in three core stories:

- The Origin Story — Why did this begin? Who saw the need? What friction or pain point demanded change? This is the emotional seed. It makes the effort relatable.

- The Impact Story — What tangible shift did it create? Who was helped? Where did it succeed— and where did it struggle? This is the story that builds belief.

- The Future Story — What could this become? What larger mission does it serve? How does each person play a role in sustaining it? This is the story that recruits ownership.

Narrative intelligence is not the domain of marketing. It's a strategic capability. Leaders must be trained to report outcomes and frame them with meaning. Data shows that stories activate more areas of the brain than facts alone— particularly those associated with emotion and memory. In a world overwhelmed with dashboards, the story becomes the differentiator.

At SummitCare, leadership embedded storytelling into their quarterly operational reviews. Instead of jumping straight to metrics, every report opened with a real story— of a patient who helped, a clinician who improvised, or a team that rebounded from failure. This wasn't sentimentality. It was strategy. It reminded every leader in the room why the numbers mattered.

Scaling initiatives without stories is like building roads without signs. You might reach your destination, but no one will remember the journey.

Narrative intelligence ensures that transformation isn't just delivered.

It's understood, felt, and passed on.

Institutionalize Listening as a Strategy

Organizations that scale well don't just push—they receive. Listening isn't just a feel-good gesture. It's a strategic advantage. As complexity rises, feedback becomes the early detection system for friction, fatigue, or failure. Yet too often, listening is treated as episodic—something done after rollout, through surveys or town halls. Visionary organizations embed it into the fabric of scaling itself.

At Evergreen Health, every scaled program includes a "listening lab"—a rotating feedback mechanism that brings frontline voices into strategic decisions. Tools include:

- Weekly anonymous micro-polls on implementation friction
- Story walls: a space for team members to post real experiences
- 'Voice Circles': biweekly sessions where feedback is coded and themed, then shared upward

But Evergreen didn't stop there. They created a "Feedback-to-Action Map," visible to all staff, that showed which comments had led to changes—a revised workflow, a new training module, or a shift in metrics. This simple visual proved transformational. People began to believe that their input wasn't just collected—it counted.

In another system, an internal AI tool scanned narrative feedback for emotional tone and emerging concerns. Patterns of exhaustion or confusion were flagged faster than any formal report. This combination of human and machine listening became a quiet superpower—giving leadership a real-time dashboard of cultural health.

Listening at scale requires more than a mechanism. It requires a mindset. Leaders must treat feedback not as a threat but as data, not as judgment but as a gift.

When people feel heard, they invest. When they invest, they own. And when they own, transformation takes root—not just at launch, but for the long haul.

Because in a scaled system, the distance between strategy and reality grows. Listening is how we close that gap.

It's how we lead with humility—and adapt with precision.

Rebuild for Connection, Not Just Capacity

As healthcare systems scale, it's easy to focus on logistics: more beds, software, and staff. But what sustains impact is not capacity. It's a connection.

One children's hospital built a new satellite campus with cutting-edge equipment. However, early patient satisfaction scores lagged. After investigation, they found that staff felt disconnected while the buildings were state-of-the-art. Relationships hadn't caught up with infrastructure.

Leadership responded by launching a cross-campus immersion initiative—staff from the original site rotated through the new facility weekly. Peer-to-peer mentorship was formalized. A shared storytelling platform was introduced.

Six months later, satisfaction rose—and so did collaboration, retention, and innovation.

Connection isn't sentimental. It's structural. It's what lets scale feel human.

Scientific Insight: The Neuroscience of Belonging

Emerging neuroscience confirms what visionary leaders have long intuited: Belonging is not a soft concept—it's a powerful neurobiological driver of performance, innovation, and resilience. When individuals feel psychologically safe and socially connected, the brain releases oxytocin, dopamine, and serotonin—neurochemicals that enhance trust, motivation, and well-being.

The prefrontal cortex, responsible for executive functioning and decision-making, is significantly more active when people feel seen, heard, and valued. Conversely, when individuals think excluded or uncertain about their place in a system, the brain activates threat responses that impair cognition, creativity, and collaboration. As described in studies by UCLA neuroscientist Dr. Matthew Lieberman, social pain—like exclusion—registers in the brain similarly to physical pain. The implications for scaling organizations are profound.

When scaling with soul, leaders must intentionally design systems that support these neurobiological truths. It's not just about better morale. It's about building cognitive capacity and adaptive intelligence across the workforce.

Here's how we do it:

- **Recognition Rituals**: Publicly acknowledging behaviors aligned with the mission, especially during times of change. Recognition activates reward circuits and reinforces identity alignment.
- **Choice Architecture:** Involving staff in implementation decisions improves adoption and engages the anterior cingulate cortex, a region

associated with conflict resolution and cognitive empathy.

- **Emotional Check-ins**: Brief, structured moments in team huddles or meetings where people can express how they process change. This validates emotional reality and improves oxytocin levels, strengthening group trust.

These strategies are backed by research from Stanford, MIT, and the Neuro Leadership Institute, all pointing to the same truth: Belonging fuels performance, not as an HR initiative but as a neurological imperative.

When we scale with empathy, we scale brainpower. When we design for trust, we unlock innovation.

When leaders make the brain feel safe, the organization becomes bold.

That's not sentiment. That's science.

Conclusion: Grow Like a Forest, Not a Factory

Factories replicate. Forests regenerate. They grow by respecting their roots, diversifying their reach, and adjusting to each new environment with wisdom. In healthcare, we often design for mechanical growth—add clinics, replicate programs, and expand access. However, an accurate scale in a purpose-driven system must be more like ecological growth: organic, intelligent, and responsive.

Healthcare systems that scale with soul understand this. They don't measure growth just by volume—but by vitality. Like forests, they maintain a living memory. They regenerate leadership through mentorship. They recycle experience into wisdom. They absorb shocks like pandemics or staffing crises—through cultural resilience, not just operational redundancy.

They understand that the richness of the ecosystem matters. A forest thrives not because every tree is identical but because its biodiversity sustains its strength. Similarly, scaled systems must allow local variation, frontline voice, and community wisdom to remain alive even as enterprise infrastructure provides support and coherence.

Think of scale not as horizontal expansion but as vertical deepening. Every new layer should reinforce the foundational values, not dilute them. The best systems grow tall because their roots go deep.

As a CEO or visionary leader, your role is not just to build the factory. It is to tend the forest. To nourish soil - culture, trust, and purpose. To prune what no longer serves. To plant for futures, you may never see.

Because the actual scale test doesn't show how fast you grow.

It's how whole you remain.

And if you build systems where empathy expands with size, connection deepens with complexity, and the story drives strategy, scale isn't a threat to the soul.

It's how you keep it alive.

It's how you build a legacy that breathes.

Chapter 7: The Future-Ready System

Section 1: Designing for Agility and Alignment

The future will not reward the most prominent systems. It will reward the most agile ones.

In a healthcare landscape of volatility, value-based care, consumer expectations, and workforce transformation, agility isn't a buzzword—it's a survival trait. But agility without Alignment becomes chaos. To lead in tomorrow's healthcare economy, systems must master the capacity to move quickly and the clarity to move together.

This section explores how visionary leaders design future-ready organizations—not by chasing trends but by building structural agility and cultural coherence into the very bones of the system. Agility becomes not an afterthought but a leadership posture. Alignment becomes not just about consensus but coherence across every enterprise level.

Static Models vs. Strategic Elasticity

Healthcare operated under a legacy paradigm for too long: long-range plans, rigid budgets, and siloed departments. These systems assumed stability, predictability, and linear growth. In that model, five-year strategies were locked in binders, updated annually at best, and often disconnected from the pace of change in clinical care, technology, or market dynamics.

But the pandemic—and the digital acceleration that followed—exposed a painful truth: Those systems couldn't turn fast enough. *They were like cargo ships trying to navigate rapids.*

Future-ready systems pivot, not panic. They recognize that the environment is not just changing—it's continuously evolving. To survive and thrive, they embed strategic elasticity into their architecture: a leadership philosophy and operating model that allows organizations to stretch, flex, and respond to disruption without breaking.

Strategic elasticity means:

- **Short-cycle planning:** The Strategy is updated quarterly or monthly based on real-time data.
- **Modular budgeting:** Capital and operational spending are structured in tiers, allowing funds to shift quickly to high-impact areas.

- **Scenario playbooks:** Organizations proactively model out multiple future scenarios and rehearse responses before crisis strikes.

At Harmony Health, executives replaced the traditional five-year planning cycle with a "**living strategy model**." Every 90 days, cross-functional teams gather to revisit assumptions, evaluate market shifts, and reassign resources. When a new retail health competitor emerged in their region, they didn't convene a crisis task force—they were already running playbook scenarios. Within six weeks, they launched a countering virtual-first service line.

This is agility by design—not accident.

Elasticity also means building talent systems that match the strategic rhythm. At VitalOne Health, staffing plans are updated based on real-time patient volume, and teams are trained in dual-skill roles to enable internal mobility. Workforce planning is no longer an annual HR activity— it's a strategic lever.

In future-ready organizations, agility is not reactionary. It's rhythmic. It becomes part of the muscle memory of the system, allowing teams to shift quickly while staying grounded in the mission.

The Strategic Alignment Triangle

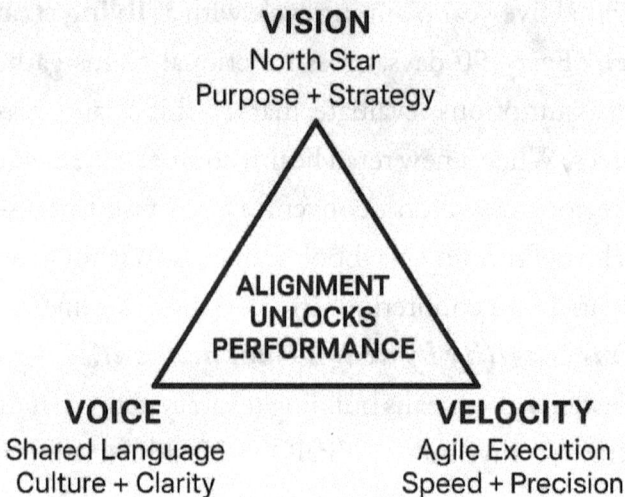

VISION
North Star
Purpose + Strategy

ALIGNMENT
UNLOCKS
PERFORMANCE

VOICE
Shared Language
Culture + Clarity

VELOCITY
Agile Execution
Speed + Precision

Aligning Vision, Voice, and Velocity

Speed without clarity creates confusion. Alignment without speed breeds irrelevance. In a fast-moving healthcare environment, where disruption can come from new technologies, policy shifts, or unexpected crises, the true power lies in achieving coordinated acceleration—organizations that move swiftly because they move together.

Future-ready systems align three critical forces:

- Vision sets the long-term direction. It answers: Where are we headed and why? It provides the North Star for both strategic decisions and daily behaviors.
- Voice reflects the shared language and cultural norms that guide behavior across teams. When people use common frameworks to discuss problems and priorities, collaboration accelerates.
- Velocity determines how quickly an organization can respond to disruption without losing coherence or diluting impact.

Transformation doesn't feel like disruption when all three align—it feels like evolution.

At Horizon Regional, a shift toward a digital-first strategy was achieved in under six months, not because of brute executive force but because the groundwork had already been laid. Their strategic vision had been communicated through immersive leadership forums and translated into local team narratives. Their "One Voice Playbook" gave every department a shared vocabulary for framing challenges, decisions, and risks. Staff had pre-established "velocity parameters"—guardrails defining where autonomy began and coordination was needed.

The result? Rapid alignment without chaos. Decentralized execution with centralized purpose.

This model isn't theory—it's muscle memory built through deliberate practice. Alignment becomes a reflex, not a reaction.

Organizations that struggle with scale often conflate communication with alignment. But proper alignment goes deeper. It's not about cascading memos. It's about cascading meaning.

Future-ready systems ensure that whether someone is leading strategy in a boardroom or triaging patients in a hallway, they are making decisions from the same playbook—and moving toward the same horizon.

This is what it means to design alignment as a capability, not a coincidence.

Structural Design: From Hierarchies to Ecosystems

Traditional healthcare hierarchies are brittle. Decision-making is slow. Innovation is bottlenecked. And frontlines often feel disconnected from those shaping enterprise strategy. These top-down structures, born in the industrial age, are optimized for control—not adaptability.

However, the complexity of modern healthcare demands something different: resilient and regenerative systems. Enter the ecosystem model—a design philosophy that trades linear chains of command for dynamic webs of collaboration.

Future-ready systems reimagine themselves as distributed, decentralized, and deeply interconnected ecosystems. Rather than organizing by function or department, they design around value streams—the pathways through which patient needs are met, outcomes are delivered, and impact is generated.

This transformation unlocks several advantages:

- Faster Decision-Making at the Edge: Empowering those closest to the problem to make decisions. Nurses, care coordinators, and IT analysts no longer need executive permission to fix what's broken—they have agency within aligned parameters.

- Greater Cross-Disciplinary Collaboration: Teams aren't built around titles—they're built around purpose. A behavioral health innovation team might include a psychiatrist, a community health worker, a data scientist, and a facilities planner—all working toward one shared outcome.

- Clear Accountability Without Micromanagement: Ecosystem models operate on clear metrics and mutual trust. Success isn't about hours clocked or emails sent—it's about progress toward shared objectives.

One progressive system created a Care Transformation Network—a constellation of multidisciplinary teams embedded in each region. Each team had budgetary authority, strategic autonomy, and a direct reporting line to the enterprise transformation office. They weren't pilot factories. They were full-fledged innovation engines.

But ecosystem design doesn't mean anarchy. It means intentional architecture:

- Strategic connective tissue—shared language, integrated data systems, and aligned incentives
- Minimal viable bureaucracy—just enough structure to support agility, not stifle it
- Leadership as stewardship—guiding and enabling rather than commanding and controlling

This is not just an operational redesign. It's a **philosophical shift—from managing people to empowering potential.**

And in that shift, systems don't just flatten. They flourish.

Building a Culture of Constructive Disruption

Agile alignment isn't just structural—it's cultural. A rigid process cannot produce nimbleness. Only a courageous, feedback-rich culture can. In future-ready healthcare systems, disruption is no longer a threat—it's a discipline. And building a culture that embraces it starts with dismantling the fear of failure.

Constructive disruption requires three things:

- Psychological safety: People must know that speaking up—even with bad news—is valued.
- Rewarding risk: Innovation must be incentivized, not just tolerated.

- Ritualized reflection: Teams need time and space to learn from successes and setbacks.

At ElevateCare, leadership institutionalized a "fail-forward framework." Every quarter, leaders highlight initiatives that didn't meet targets—but are celebrated for bold thinking, transparency, and iterative learning. One story involved a predictive staffing tool that produced only modest improvements. But the team behind it was promoted—not penalized—for pioneering a system that now informs a broader AI pilot.

They also introduced Innovation Labs—safe zones where frontline staff could test micro-changes without extensive approvals. A nurse-led project redesigned shift handoffs using color-coded dashboards. It reduced communication errors by 18% in four months and scaled across four hospitals.

Crucially, the language around failure changed. Instead of post-mortems, ElevateCare holds "growth reviews." Instead of quarterly business reviews that obsess over perfection, they spotlight learning velocity.

This rebranding of disruption builds a leadership mindset where change is embraced, not endured. And that cultural mindset ripples across the system.

One of their CMOs summarized it this way: *"Our goal isn't to get every innovation right. It's to get every team confident they can try again."*

In environments like these, innovation becomes consistent—not chaotic. Teams don't wait for permission. They act with purpose. And that's the kind of culture where disruption isn't just managed—it's mastered.

Conclusion: Blueprint for a Moving System

The healthcare system of the future is not a rigid structure—it's a living organism. It breathes, adapts, and grows. Its strength is not in how well it holds its shape but in how effectively it reshapes itself with intention, clarity, and speed.

Designing for agility and alignment requires more than structural adjustments. It calls for visionary leadership—leaders who understand that today's strategy must be elastic, culture must be scalable, and disruption must be welcomed as a form of innovation.

Agility is not about endless change. It's about purposeful movement. Alignment is not conformity—it's coherence across purpose, people, and performance. When the two are built into the architecture of an organization, transformation becomes a system property, not just a leadership initiative.

These organizations don't pause to shift—they pivot by design. They foster shared language across every level, operationalize listening, and flatten hierarchies without losing accountability. They scale not because they expand quickly but because they scale wisely—with empathy, foresight, and clarity of intent.

And ultimately, they do more than survive disruption—they metabolize it into strength.

Because in a world where the future changes by the week, the only systems that will survive are those designed to evolve.

And the only leaders who will thrive are those bold enough to reimagine not just care delivery—but the very DNA of the organization itself.

The blueprint isn't static. It's alive.

It's not a roadmap, it's a rhythm.

Section 2: Integrated Care Models That Work

The phrase "integrated care" is everywhere, but its meaning is often shallow, fragmented, or lost in HR white papers. Proper integration isn't about communication between departments or surface-level referrals. It's about building a cohesive, longitudinal, and value-driven ecosystem where the patient experience, clinical outcomes, and operational efficiency align seamlessly.

This section explores what real integration looks like in future-ready systems. We go beyond buzzwords to examine structural, financial, and technological elements that make integrated care scalable—and sustainable.

Beyond Coordination: Designing for Clinical Unity

Most systems claim to coordinate care. Fewer integrate it. Coordination implies communication; integration demands transformation. Integration means collapsing silos—not just of data but of decision-making, accountability, workflow, and incentives. It means replacing sequential care with synchronous care—where primary care, behavioral health, specialty services, and even social supports function as one integrated unit, not as loosely affiliated contacts.

At Clarion Integrated Health, the commitment to clinical unity began with physical infrastructure but extended to performance design. Rather than treating behavioral health as an ancillary referral, Clarion embedded full-time licensed behavioral health clinicians in every primary care setting. But the real innovation wasn't in the co-location. It was in how these teams were empowered to practice: they attended daily huddles with primary care teams, used a shared clinical record, and—most critically—were held to the same quality and outcome measures.

This wasn't a pilot. It was an operational mandate.

Even more compelling, Clarion eliminated separate performance dashboards. Whether a patient was managing diabetes or depression, their care journey lived on a single platform with unified goals—screening adherence, functional improvement, medication compliance, and patient satisfaction. Clinical unity didn't require everyone to agree, but it required everyone to be accountable to the same truth.

The result? Improved clinical outcomes, shorter time to intervention, and higher patient engagement. But perhaps more importantly, it built trust—across teams and with patients. When your care doesn't feel like handoffs between disconnected experts, it feels like healing.

This is not co-location. It's co-creation. Co-ownership. Co-responsibility.

And in the future-ready system, it's the only care that will last.

Technology as a Platform, Not a Patch

Integrated care cannot exist without interoperable, real-time data systems. But technology alone won't solve fragmentation. The most innovative systems treat technology as a strategic enabler—not a compliance tool, digital filing cabinet, and indeed not a one-time project. They see it as the nervous system of integrated care— transmitting signals, connecting organs, and enabling reflexes.

At NovaCare Alliance, integration started by building a tech architecture that followed the patient—not the provider. Instead of forcing workflows to bend around legacy systems, they developed a longitudinal care platform that aggregated structured and unstructured data from EHRs, home monitoring devices, social determinants databases, and pharmacy records. This data didn't just sit in dashboards—it drove action.

AI and predictive analytics flagged clinical deterioration or gaps in care before symptoms surfaced. A patient managing heart failure and depression might trigger a team alert not because they missed an appointment but because their engagement patterns on the mobile app changed and their biometric readings from a home device shifted. Technology enabled preemptive empathy.

What set NovaCare apart wasn't the sophistication of its tools—it was how seamlessly those tools were embedded into human workflows. Care teams had real-time visibility into patients' needs, goals, and risks. Providers spent less time documenting and more time connecting. Even family caregivers had controlled access to coordination portals.

Moreover, digital platforms were designed around the patient's story, not the organization's structure. A person wasn't toggling between siloed portals for cardiology, endocrinology, and behavioral health. They interacted with one system that saw them as a whole person—longitudinally, contextually, and compassionately.

Proper integration happens when digital infrastructure mirrors the human journey. When tech stops being a patch and becomes the platform, care delivery moves from fragmented transactions to orchestrated experiences.

That is the technological soul of a truly integrated health system.

Reimbursement Alignment: Value Must Travel

You can't integrate care with disintegrated payment models. Financial incentives shape behavior. If those incentives reward volume over value and siloed transactions over shared outcomes, even the most visionary clinical models will falter.

Future-ready systems don't just redesign care delivery—they reengineer how it's paid for. The goal is to create payment models that travel with the patient—supporting continuity, coordination, and shared responsibility across providers, services, and sites.

At NorthAxis Health, the shift began with a simple question: What if we stopped reimbursing services and started investing in outcomes? Their answer was the launch of bundled payments for procedures or chronic conditions and life journeys. One standout model was their integrated maternity pathway. Rather than billing separately for obstetrics, behavioral health, nutrition counseling, and postpartum support, they developed a single financial construct that funded the entire continuum of maternal care.

The impact was immediate. Silos dissolved. Obstetricians collaborated daily with social workers. Mental health screenings became routine, not optional. Patients received personalized care plans, and care teams jointly owned the journey's success—from the first prenatal visit to twelve months postpartum.

This wasn't just about cost containment. It was about economic Alignment. Integration becomes embedded, not episodic, when everyone is incentivized to support the whole person.

Other systems are advancing, such as adopting population-based capitation models that include behavioral, dental, pharmacy, and housing supports. These aren't financial experiments. They are strategic infrastructure blueprints for resilience in a value-based future.

To make integration real, value must move fluidly. Through systems. Across settings. And most importantly—around the patient.

Only when the money moves with the mission can care genuinely come together.

Operational Governance: Integrated Means Accountable

Integrated care requires integrated governance. Without structural accountability, integration devolves into wishful thinking—discussed at strategy retreats but rarely felt at the front lines. Future-ready systems build governance models where responsibility doesn't just span departments—it binds them.

This begins with leadership architecture. At Equinox Health, interdisciplinary leadership councils were formed not as advisory groups but as empowered decision-making bodies. These councils include representatives from finance, operations, clinical services, digital infrastructure, and population health. Their mandate? To drive unified performance, use shared metrics and transparent dashboards that reflect system-wide outcomes, not siloed successes.

These are not cross-functional meetings for consensus—they are executive task forces with enterprise authority. Their metrics include medication adherence, avoidable ED utilization, access equity, longitudinal patient engagement, and outcomes for specific cohorts (e.g., high-risk maternal health and multimorbidity in seniors).

Accountability flows both vertically and horizontally. Site-based leaders report into matrixed structures that include service line executives and system integration officers. Frontline innovations are fast-tracked when they align with integrated KPIs—and leaders are evaluated not just on budget performance but on their ability to eliminate fragmentation.

Governance extends to board-level oversight. Equinox created a Strategic Integration Committee at the enterprise level—a board subcommittee focused on how care, technology, and experience come together. This group reviews clinical and financial outcomes with a specific lens: Did this pathway reduce fragmentation? Did it improve coherence for the patient?

In this structure, integration becomes more than a strategic narrative. It becomes the scaffolding of daily operations.

That's the point—because until accountability is shared, integration will remain a philosophy.

However, when governance is genuinely integrated, care becomes accountable to the only outcome that matters: the patient's lived experience.

Conclusion: Don't Just Integrate—Orchestrate

The next era of healthcare will be defined not by how many services you offer but by how well they connect. Integration is not the end goal—it's the operating system for continuity, efficiency, and trust.

Future-ready systems don't simply connect departments—they compose symphonies of care. They replace handoffs with harmonies. They understand that a patient's journey should not feel like moving from one disconnected soloist to the next but like a unified performance where every team knows the melody.

And as systems evolve, the winners won't be those with the most locations or largest EHRs. They'll be those who turn integration into orchestration—where every part of the enterprise plays in harmony toward outcomes that matter.

This orchestration is not about perfection. It's about presence. It's about seeing the patient not as a case but as a continuum—across time, disciplines, and experiences.

Because in tomorrow's health system, the conductor isn't the executive. It's the design. And the sheet music is written with empathy, accountability, and aligned intent.

"Integrated care isn't just a framework—it's a frequency. And only those systems that learn to tune into the whole human experience will remain resonant in the future of health."

— **Sumit Sharma**

That's what makes integrated care work.

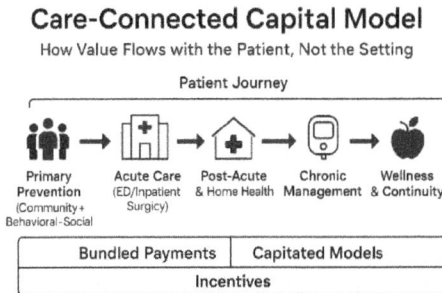

Care-Connected Capital Model
How Value Flows with the Patient, Not the Setting

Patient Journey

| Primary Prevention (Community + Behavioral-Social) | Acute Care (ED/Inpatient Surgicy) | Post-Acute & Home Health | Chronic Management | Wellness & Continuity |

| Bundled Payments | Capitated Models |
| Incentives | |

Section 3: Digitally Enabled, Human-Driven Infrastructure

Technology alone will not save healthcare. But without it, transformation is impossible.

The future of healthcare infrastructure is not about more apps or newer machines—it's about weaving digital and physical systems into a seamless, intelligent, and intuitive ecosystem. The winning systems of tomorrow will use technology not to replace the human touch but to amplify it.

This section explores how health systems can build digitally enabled, human-driven infrastructure that is scalable, flexible, and centered around the lived experience of patients and clinicians.

From Digital Exhaust to Digital Intelligence

Most health systems today produce data as a byproduct—what technologists call digital exhaust. EHR entries, billing codes, scheduling logs, and patient portal clicks. But very few systems know how to transform that exhaust into intelligence.

Future-ready systems reimagine their digital architecture as an insight engine. They use AI, machine learning, and natural language processing to convert unstructured data into actionable insights. Clinical notes become care signals. Missed appointments become risk alerts. Voice interactions become experienced data.

At Sentinel Health, this shift was strategic. They implemented an enterprise AI layer above their core systems, continuously analyzing real-time clinical, operational, and engagement data. The insights don't live in dashboards—they are routed directly into clinician workflows. A nurse receives a real-time prompt when a patient's pattern matches early-stage sepsis. A care coordinator is alerted when transportation issues might jeopardize follow-up compliance.

Human-Centered Design as a Strategic Mandate

Tech adoption in healthcare often fails because the end user—be it a patient or provider—was never consulted. Buttons are in the wrong place. Alerts are overwhelming. Interfaces assume medical literacy or tech fluency. This is not transformation. It's the transference of burden. And that burden manifests as burnout, disengagement, and costly workarounds.

Human-centered design (HCD) isn't about aesthetics or convenience. It's a strategic discipline rooted in empathy, systems thinking, and iterative problem-solving. The best systems don't treat HCD as a UX project—they embed it into the innovation lifecycle, operational governance, and enterprise culture.

At Horizon Systems, human-centered design begins at the strategic planning table. Every major tech deployment is preceded by co-design labs involving patients, nurses, physicians, IT engineers, and even environmental services staff. These labs don't ask participants to react to a finished product—they invite them to shape it. Workflows are modeled, stress-tested, broken, and rebuilt—before a single line of code goes live.

Their design team created simulation environments where real users walk through new tools in near-live scenarios, providing instant feedback to redesign navigation, language, alert timing, and accessibility features. In one case, this process led to overhauling a medication reconciliation tool that cut documentation time by 42% and improved accuracy.

But the impact goes deeper. By honoring lived experience, Horizon builds trust in transformation. Clinicians feel seen. Patients feel respected. And digital tools become invisible partners in care—not barriers to it.

This process is not just about usability. It's about dignity. It's about designing not for users but with them. Because when you build with empathy, you don't just get better adoption—you create better systems.

In a future-ready infrastructure, human-centered design isn't a feature. It's the foundation.

Digital Infrastructure that Scales Across the Enterprise

Point solutions are the enemy of progress. A scheduling app and a remote monitoring pilot are here, but there are no scales if the underlying architecture is fragmented. The future-ready system must be connected, intelligent, and resilient like a digital nervous system.

Enterprise digital infrastructure must be unified, modular, and open. Unified so data moves seamlessly with the patient across care settings. Modular so capabilities evolve incrementally without requiring costly system overhauls. Such new technologies and third-party innovations can be opened without months of vendor-specific engineering.

NorthStar Health built its infrastructure using a "digital backbone" approach. Their foundation was designed with interoperability first, not last. All core systems—EHR, analytics, scheduling, and patient engagement tools—connect through a standard API layer. Before any new platform is approved, it must prove its compatibility with this ecosystem.

However, the brilliance of NorthStar's strategy lies in its governance model. Instead of allowing department-level tech procurement, they instituted an enterprise digital council that evaluates new tools based on scalability, integration potential, and user impact. As a result, innovation became standardized. Every tool added value to the whole.

The backbone approach doesn't stifle innovation—it protects it. Teams across clinical, IT, and operations know that new solutions won't break the system. They'll expand it.

Equally important is how infrastructure supports the clinician and patient experience. A single patient ID links every interaction—from hospital stays to text reminders to virtual visits. A care manager doesn't have to log into five systems to track engagement. A physician sees a single dashboard that blends clinical data with social risk factors.

The experience feels continuous—not cobbled. Strategic—not accidental. Human—not transactional.

In an era of transformation fatigue and technology overload, the systems that scale sustainably build digital with discipline. Because agility doesn't come from plugging in more tools but from architecting with intention.

Conclusion: Tech as the Conduit, Not the Destination

The most potent infrastructure doesn't compete with humanity—it elevates it. Technology becomes the invisible scaffolding that supports trust, communication, and healing in the future-ready system.

It senses what's needed. It steps aside when not. It moves data so people can move with empathy.

And the systems that get this right will stop chasing digital transformation—and start leading human transformation.

These ideas don't live in a lab. They live in the gray space between design and deployment, strategy and execution. They require leaders who understand both workflows and wisdom. Leaders who know that care shines in the foreground when infrastructure hums quietly in the background.

This isn't about building from the outside. It's about evolving what we already have—carefully, thoughtfully, and with strategic intent.

Because while technology may enable the system, only people can evolve it. The next transformation era requires leaders to bridge the chasm between digital systems and human experience—translating complexity into clarity and strategy into trust.

"The real work of transformation isn't loud. It's quiet, structural, and deeply human. We don't need more disruption—we need infrastructure that listens, adapts, and lasts."

— **Sumit Sharma**

Section 4: Creating Strategic Flexibility and Financial Sustainability

In a world of constant disruption, financial sustainability is no longer about static cost-cutting or reactive budget cycles. It's about building systems that can flex—strategically, operationally, and economically—without breaking mission or momentum.

Healthcare leaders must stop treating financial resilience and care quality as trade-offs. They are interdependent. Strategic flexibility is the architecture that allows both to thrive. This is not just a finance function—it's a leadership imperative that connects enterprise vision with operational execution.

This section explores how future-ready systems build adaptive financial strategies that protect purpose, fuel transformation, and ensure long-term viability—even in turbulent markets.

Goodbye to Linear Planning

Traditional five-year plans are relics of a stable past. Today's leaders face a landscape where payer mix, workforce dynamics, supply chains, and competitive threats can shift in months—not decades. Linear thinking traps organizations in outdated assumptions.

Strategic flexibility begins by embracing non-linear, scenario-based planning. At Equinox Health, financial planning is no longer a once-a-year ritual—it's a rolling process. Strategy and finance teams meet quarterly to update assumptions, re-prioritize capital, and reallocate operating funds based on real-time indicators. What used to be a fixed budget is now a responsive investment portfolio.

This isn't chaos. It's agility with guardrails.

Scenario modeling includes multiple future states: regulatory shifts, competitor moves, volume volatility, and workforce availability. Each scenario has pre-defined response plans. When inflation surged, and travel nurse rates spiked, Equinox executed their workforce flexibility scenario within 10 days—protecting quality while mitigating cost exposure.

Organizations like Polaris Health have added digital simulation tools to these processes—allowing leadership teams to interact with their models in real-time. CFOs and COOs test decisions together, not in sequence. Strategic questions like "What happens if we delay CapEx on facility expansion and shift to virtual hubs?" can be answered instantly.

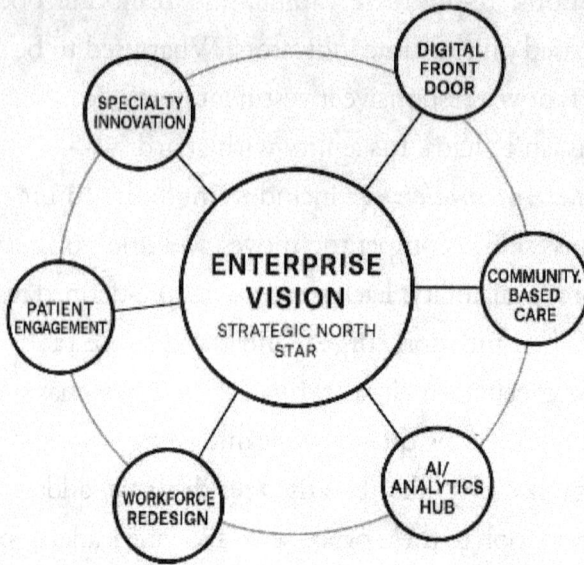

The future doesn't wait. Neither should planning.

Strategic Cost Intelligence

Cutting costs is easy. Sustaining value while optimizing cost is leadership.

Forward-looking systems are shifting from blunt cost containment to precision cost intelligence. They build real-time cost accounting systems that connect every dollar to a clinical pathway, patient segment, or strategic objective.

At MeridianCare, financial teams partnered with operations to build a dynamic cost-to-serve model. Rather than relying on outdated cost reports, leaders could see—

in near real-time—the cost per encounter for every service line, broken down by fixed and variable components. This model guided decisions such as when to outsource, redesign workflows, and reinvest.

But future-ready cost intelligence doesn't stop at tracking spend—it enables yield optimization. Healthcare systems are now borrowing from industries like aviation and logistics to apply yield management principles, maximizing return on limited capacity by aligning demand, timing, and value.

One system, AxisHealth, built a yield-based OR scheduling model. By analyzing surgeon performance, case complexity, length-of-stay predictions, and reimbursement yield, they could allocate block time by volume and strategic contribution—this improved revenue by 9% without adding a new OR or clinician.

Yield-based thinking is also transforming inpatient throughput, imaging, and infusion services. Leaders no longer ask, "How much does it cost?" They ask, "What is the return on this capacity, and how do we increase its strategic contribution?"

Clinical leaders received cost transparency dashboards tied to quality outcomes. Instead of being viewed as an afterthought, cost became part of care design. Surgeons at MeridianCare now lead quarterly reviews with finance partners to identify high-cost variations and align resource use with outcomes—not just volume.

Strategic cost intelligence means money doesn't just track operations—it informs transformation. And with yield-based principles in play, it doesn't just optimize cost—it amplifies value.

Flexing CapEx and OpEx with Purpose

Rigid capital planning kills innovation. Future-ready systems rethink the boundary between capital and operating expenses to support scalable experimentation, innovation at the edge, and timely response to market conditions.

Traditional budgeting processes treat CapEx as long-term, fixed commitments and OpEx as tightly controlled day-to-day costs. However, in future-ready enterprises, both are reframed as dynamic strategic growth levers.

Consider this: At Polaris Health, 15% of their innovation budget is deliberately left unallocated at the start of the fiscal year. These funds are governed by an Innovation Council that can deploy capital mid-cycle to fund high-impact ideas emerging from frontline teams or sudden shifts in market demand. This approach reflects a shift from rigid approval hierarchies to responsive capital stewardship.

Polaris also employs an adaptive capital allocation model based on iterative business cases. Innovation proposals are not funded all at once but through stage-gated releases. Teams must demonstrate traction or early wins before accessing the next round of investment—

mimicking venture capital principles inside a healthcare enterprise.

On the OpEx side, Polaris established a portfolio-based model where initiatives are grouped by strategic value, not departmental ownership. Each initiative must define its return: clinical, financial, operational, or reputational. This allows leaders to make trade-offs across portfolios, not just within silos.

Strategic flexibility also requires new financial language. Instead of "capital spending," systems discuss "strategic optionality." Instead of just "budget variances," they focus on "learning margins"—how much they invest in discovery versus delivery.

Yield-based metrics are also applied here. If a mobile clinic costs $500,000 in CapEx but improves preventive visit yield by 23%, that spend isn't just justified—it's optimized. When leaders think of capital as capacity investment, not just infrastructure, the ROI lens becomes expansive.

This disciplined flexibility turns budgeting into strategy—not just accounting. It positions finance not as a gatekeeper but as a growth partner capable of fueling rapid innovation while maintaining fiscal accountability.

Funding the Future Without Mortgaging It

Bold transformation requires bold investment. But it cannot be funded with naive optimism or short-term gains. Future-ready systems must learn to balance visionary ambition with financial discipline—to bet on the future without borrowing too heavily against it.

Forward-thinking systems identify "mission-aligned revenue"—business lines or partnerships that generate income without compromising clinical standards, workforce well-being, or brand trust. At Lumina Health, this includes virtual second opinions, direct-to-employer care partnerships, and digital therapeutics platforms. Revenue from these ventures is not siphoned off to plug budget gaps—it is reinvested in high-leverage assets: workforce upskilling, predictive analytics platforms, and community health infrastructure.

Lumina and others are leaning into capital innovation to fund big moves without financial overexposure. Joint ventures, co-development agreements, and public-private partnerships are on the rise. Lumina's flagship virtual care expansion was funded through a three-way collaboration with a health tech startup and a regional broadband provider—spreading cost, risk, and benefit. These models allow systems to stretch faster—without mortgaging their balance sheet.

Another powerful lever is a philanthropic investment with strategic intent. Rather than treating philanthropy as a charity, future-ready systems use it to seed innovation. At Unity Health, donor funds launched a $10 million AI-driven social determinants pilot—framed as a platform for future enterprise-scale work. These dollars are catalytic, not just symbolic.

Crucially, these systems apply a dual-lens ROI framework. One lens focuses on traditional financial metrics: margins, EBITDA, and cost per case. The other focuses on strategic relevance: Does this initiative position us competitively for value-based care? Does it deepen our relationship with underserved populations? Does it build capability we will need 5–10 years from now?

Some innovations will not pay off this quarter—or even next year. But their strategic return is undeniable. And the wisest leaders know that not every seed becomes a harvest overnight.

The art is in knowing when to plant when to prune, and when to double down. Because funding the future isn't about taking risks—it's about designing them.

Conclusion: Build Elasticity Into the Balance Sheet

Resilience is not reactive—it's designed. Financial sustainability in healthcare isn't about austerity. It's about elasticity. It's the ability to flex funding, recalibrate priorities, and deploy resources with clarity and speed—regardless of whether the challenge is a pandemic, a recession, or a policy shift.

Leaders must navigate organizational complexity and the broader currents of macro and microeconomics to build elasticity. Shifting interest rates, labor market volatility, and inflationary pressure demand real-time modeling and hedging strategies at the macro level. A system that ignores macroeconomic signals becomes reactive. A system that reads them wisely becomes predictive.

At the microeconomic level, elasticity aligns incentives, marginal cost structures, and behavioral economics with enterprise goals. Understanding how clinicians make choices, how patients respond to pricing and engagement strategies, and how resource scarcity impacts productivity allows financial models to reflect reality—not just projections.

Systems that thrive will embed financial strategy into the rhythm of operations, where every budget cycle is a strategic dialogue, where every dollar has direction. Finance teams are co-creators of the future, not guardians of the past. And where elasticity is not just a fiscal posture—but a cultural one.

Because the **next wave of disruption won't send a calendar invite**, it will show up fast, noisy, and unforgiving. And the systems that last will be the ones already moving—already flexing—already ready.

The Culture Change Curve

How Mindsets Evolve from Resistance to Ownership

Embedding
"It feels natural now"

Practice
"We're allowed to try"

Permission
"You're allowed to try"

Resistance
"That's not how
we do things"

Section 5: The Operating System of the Future

There is no future without a new operating system for healthcare—one that is not just digital but dynamic. Not just efficient but evolutionary. Not just integrated but intelligent.

The operating system drives scale, agility, and innovation in every other high-performing industry. Healthcare, historically burdened by legacy processes and siloed execution, now stands at the edge of a structural breakthrough. But it will take visionary leadership to redefine how we think, work, and build in a post-industrial care economy.

This section imagines what the operating system of a genuinely future-ready healthcare system looks like—and what strategic leaders must do to create it.

From Linear Pipelines to Adaptive Platforms

Legacy systems in healthcare were built like pipelines—linear processes designed to move patients from intake to discharge, with minimal iteration. These models assumed predictability: a single path, standardized steps, and one-size-fits-all interventions. That model may have sufficed in the fee-for-service era, where volume defined success. But in today's healthcare environment—characterized by chronic conditions, social determinants, behavioral nuance, and real-time digital engagement—it's no longer fit for purpose.

Pipelines break when complexity rises. What's needed now are adaptive platforms—systems that don't just move patients but learn from them. Platforms are iterative. They reconfigure themselves. They don't just execute care—they orchestrate it.

In a platform model, care is not a single transaction or visit. It's a continuous relationship where clinical insights, social context, digital touchpoints, and human preferences converge dynamically. The operating system must be designed to sense, respond, and evolve—not in cycles but in real time.

At HelixHealth, a future-focused integrated delivery network, the operating model mimics a tech platform more than a traditional hospital system. Patient journeys are segmented by predictive analytics that forecast risk and identify opportunities. Care plans adjust dynamically based on behavioral cues, patient-reported outcomes, and biometric feedback from wearables. Instead of rigid handoffs, care teams plug into shared coordination layers governed by AI-driven triage and routed by clinical logic trees.

This approach allows for personalization at scale. A patient with heart failure and food insecurity doesn't just get a medication refill—they trigger a cross-functional response that includes pharmacy, nutrition, and community health. The system becomes not just a processor but a partner.

Moreover, adaptive platforms support modularity. New capabilities—virtual care nodes, AI-based diagnostics, and mental health integrations—are added like apps to an ecosystem. This prevents digital sprawl and ensures coherence.

This isn't digitization. It's platformization. It repositions the health system from pipeline executor to intelligent orchestrator.

And it shifts the core question from "What did we do?" to "How did the system evolve in response?"

That's the mark of an accurate operating system—not a tool that moves people forward, but one that moves itself forward.

Intelligence-First, Not Tech-First

Many organizations confuse digitization with transformation. However, future-ready systems know installing tech is not the same as creating intelligence. Too many systems invest in electronic health records, patient portals, or AI tools without asking the more profound question: What does the organization need to know, and how quickly can it know?

The next-gen OS is built on an intelligence-first design. It doesn't just collect data—it synthesizes it, contextualizes it, and turns it into strategic foresight. Intelligence isn't about having more dashboards. It's about reducing noise and elevating what matters. And most importantly, it must distribute that intelligence to the edge—where clinical decisions are made, patients engage, and outcomes happen.

Imagine a system that doesn't wait for executive reviews or retrospective reports. Instead, it proactively surfaces insights, like an uptick in diabetic foot ulcers within a specific zip code. It pushes that alert to a care coordinator and podiatrist team in real-time—before complications occur. Or a system that detects scheduling inefficiencies across multiple clinics and autonomously recommends shift realignments to avoid burnout.

These are not theoretical. Leading-edge systems like Synapse Health are deploying neural network models to detect outliers and emerging patterns that human analysts would miss. Their infrastructure combines clinical AI, operational analytics, and workforce optimization tools— feeding a real-time command center that closes the loop between data and action.

However, the most crucial point is that intelligence must reflect context. A machine learning signal without clinical or social nuance risks decision failure. That's why intelligence-first design prioritizes explainability, interpretability, and ethical guardrails. Data science must serve human intent—not replace it.

These systems blur the line between planning and execution. The insight you get today influences the action you take now. This kind of anticipatory architecture enables what great leaders crave most: the ability to see around corners and act before the curve, not after it.

The best operating systems won't be defined by the quantity of technology deployed—but by how intelligently they think and how wisely they act.

Cultural Protocols Embedded in System Design

Every great OS is opinionated. It doesn't just perform—it prescribes. Future-ready operating systems don't just encode rules. They encode culture. They embed values into the everyday rhythm of operations—not as an afterthought, but as a guiding force.

Culture is not what hangs in the lobby but happens in moments of ambiguity. And in complex health systems, ambiguity is constant. When protocols are vague, and decisions are rushed, people default to habit. However, when culture is embedded into the operating system, the organization defaults to its values.

At Solara Health, their clinical OS includes prompts that ask physicians what to prescribe and how to frame it empathetically. They nudge care coordinators to check for food insecurity before scheduling follow-ups. These aren't compliance workflows. They are behavioral touchpoints rooted in the system's values—signals that the organization prioritizes empathy, equity, and trust.

These cues are not one-size-fits-all. They're informed by behavioral science, frontline co-design, and lived experience. Solara's leadership team runs biannual "culture audits"—systemwide reviews of how well digital workflows are aligned with organizational principles.

When a new EHR template unintentionally deprioritized trauma screenings, they didn't just fix the template. They changed the culture protocol that informed it.

This is cultural architecture in action—systems that don't just standardize behavior but reinforce purpose.

Leadership teams define these protocols in partnership with front-line teams, not in isolation. The goal isn't to standardize people—it's to standardize principles. The OS doesn't mandate how to care—it elevates how to lead.

When culture lives in the system, it scales without dilution. Values become operable. Identity becomes executable. And purpose becomes a function—not just a philosophy.

The OS Is the Strategy

In legacy systems, operating models were back-office. The strategy was for the boardroom. Execution was for the middle. But that wall no longer exists. In today's healthcare environment, where strategic pivots are required monthly—and sometimes daily—strategy must live within the system, not outside of it.

In the future, the OS is the strategy. It is how vision is operationalized. It is where choices about what to optimize, who to empower, and how to adapt are embedded—not on PowerPoint slides but in living, breathing architectures that inform behavior, decision rights, and prioritization.

When a health system commits to patient-centeredness, the OS translates that into dynamic scheduling models, cross-functional care teams, and experience metrics weighted alongside financial KPIs. When equity becomes a strategic pillar, the OS manifests it through real-time demographic data flows, targeted community investments, and language-aware engagement protocols.

Great leaders don't just broadcast priorities—they encode them. They ensure that frontline workflows, digital nudges, and even the cadence of daily huddles reflect the enterprise's strategic soul.

And when the OS is misaligned with strategy? It shows—promises to fall flat. Teams revert to habit. Energy dissipates because the strategy that isn't embedded is the strategy that isn't believed.

Don't ask for their mission statement if you want to know what an organization truly believes. Look at their OS.

Visionary leaders won't just lead strategy meetings. They will design the architecture where strategic intent becomes systemic behavior—and, by doing so, ensure that transformation doesn't rely on hope but on infrastructure.

Conclusion: Build Systems That Learn, Not Just Function

The most advanced operating systems don't simply execute tasks. They learn. They improve. They evolve. They generate value through speed or automation and their capacity to adapt strategically, culturally, and economically.

Healthcare has long chased transformation through tools, projects, and performance metrics. But those are fragments, not futures. True transformation will only happen when we build systems that can learn faster than the world changes—and that starts with leaders who think like architects, not just operators.

This is where system design intersects with macro and microeconomics. On a macro level, tomorrow's OS must account for labor market shifts, public policy cycles, and inflationary waves—embedding elasticity, not fragility. It must reflect decision psychology, incentive alignment, and localized variability in demand, access, and clinical behavior on a micro level. It must understand the balance between marginal cost and marginal impact. Between strategic intent and operational reality.

The actual OS of the future isn't just a digital backbone—it's a thinking framework. A learning layer. A cultural engine. It's part platform, part protocol, part compass. It will only work if leaders insist on systems that think in feedback loops, adapt gracefully, and scale without losing their souls.

That's the mindset required to lead in this next era.

And the leaders who will shape this future aren't just process engineers or digital evangelists. They are integrators of vision, architecture, economics, and humanity.

Because, in the end, the actual upgrade isn't technical. It's intellectual. It's emotional. It's systemic. It's strategic. And it's long overdue.

"We don't fix healthcare by upgrading systems. We fix it by upgrading what they stand for."

— **Sumit Sharma**

Chapter 8: Shaping the Future – Healthcare Megatrends and Strategic Foresight

Section 1: The 7 Healthcare Megatrends Reshaping the Industry

Every industry faces cycles of disruption, but healthcare is facing something more profound: a redefinition. What lies ahead is not just another wave of change but a structural rewiring of how care is delivered, funded, personalized, and governed. This transformation is not episodic. It's tectonic.

Healthcare has constantly evolved—slowly, sometimes painfully. But we are now entering an era where accelerated shifts in data, demographics, disease burden, and digital capability will drive long-term change. What used to unfold over decades is now compressing into quarters. The leadership mindset that governs the past won't sustain the future.

In this high-velocity environment, foresight is no longer a strategic luxury—it's a core responsibility. It is the difference between reacting and anticipating, between iteration and reinvention. Leaders who thrive in this future won't merely respond to trends. They'll see them early, interpret them wisely, and translate them into durable advantage.

To lead effectively through this inflection point, healthcare executives must learn to think like futurists while acting like architects. They must zoom out to identify signals and zoom in to design structures. They must see the connections between AI and empathy, consumerism and equity, and cost and culture.

This section outlines the seven healthcare megatrends reshaping the industry—and how visionary leaders must interpret, prioritize, and respond to them with urgency and intention.

This section outlines the seven healthcare megatrends reshaping the industry—and how visionary leaders must interpret, prioritize, and respond to them.

Precision Becomes the Default

The era of broad averages is over. What used to be population-wide protocols and one-size-fits-all regimens is being replaced by personalized medicine—rooted in genetics, behavior, environment, and real-time physiological feedback. With the convergence of AI-powered diagnostics, genomic sequencing, predictive analytics, and digital therapeutics, precision is not a niche—it's the new normal.

Imagine a care model where a patient's cancer treatment is based not just on the tumor's location but on its molecular fingerprint. Or a heart failure patient whose medication dosage adjusts daily based on biometric trends captured through a wearable. These are no longer theoretical. Institutions like Tempus, Color Genomics, and leading academic centers are operationalizing these ideas at scale.

Precision care also affects prevention. AI-driven tools now predict chronic disease onset years in advance based on subtle lifestyle, biometric, and social signals. Preventive medicine is shifting from broad-screening efforts to targeted early interventions tailored by medically, socially, and economically personalized risk clusters.

But with this promise comes new complexity. Leadership must contend with ethical challenges, reimbursement structures, and data governance models that were never built for this level of personalization. Genomic data raises questions of consent, data equity, and insurance fairness. Decision support tools must be explainable, not just accurate.

This also demands a fundamental redesign of infrastructure. Precision care creates massive volumes of heterogeneous data—from genomic to behavioral to social—requiring robust interoperability, storage, and real-time analytics platforms. More importantly, it requires a workforce trained in interpretation, not just execution.

Medical education will need to evolve. Clinicians must learn how to counsel patients on genetic risk, translate probabilistic models into human conversations, and co-design plans that reflect biology and values.

The takeaway is clear: Precision medicine isn't just a department. It's not just a new capability. It's a strategic paradigm—a way of thinking about care that permeates systems, workflows, technology, and training.

Healthcare leaders who embrace this shift won't just provide better care. They'll rebuild trust—by treating patients as unique individuals, not data points in an algorithm.

And in an age of fragmentation and complexity, that might be the most powerful differentiator.

The Rise of Home-Centric Care

The hospital is no longer the center of gravity. Enabled by virtual care, remote monitoring, mobile diagnostics, and hospital-at-home models, care rapidly migrates to where people live. What began as a COVID-era necessity has evolved into a long-term shift in care delivery.

Home-centric care doesn't mean lower standards—it demands new standards. Delivering chemotherapy, managing complex wound care, or monitoring cardiac patients at home requires precision logistics, digital integration, and trust-based relationships. It's a redefinition of what it means to be a care delivery organization.

Consider systems like Medically Home and Mayo Clinic's Advanced Care at Home model. They've demonstrated that high-acuity care delivered in the home can match or exceed inpatient outcomes while reducing complications and increasing satisfaction. But this shift requires more than clinical readiness. It demands operational redesign.

Home-based care introduces new complexity: supply chain agility for at-home equipment, real-time virtual coordination hubs, cybersecurity for remote monitoring devices, and workforce models that blend clinical skills with hospitality and logistics. It also challenges traditional reimbursement structures and licensing models, requiring advocacy, flexibility, and innovation at the policy level.

The implications extend beyond infrastructure. Home is an emotionally charged space—rich with meaning, family dynamics, and social determinants. Leaders must recognize that care delivered in a living room, not a clinic, alters power dynamics and redefines trust.

Access also takes on a new definition. No longer limited to miles from a hospital, access now hinges on broadband connectivity, caregiver availability, and digital literacy. Equity gaps can widen without intentional design.

Strategically, home-centric care shifts the economic model. Instead of centralizing expensive real estate and inpatient resources, systems must distribute care capabilities—scaling not through building more beds but by deploying innovative kits, platforms, and people.

The next frontier isn't remote care—it's relational care delivered locally, supported virtually, and personalized profoundly. Systems that get this right won't just improve outcomes. They'll redefine the patient experience at its most human level: at home.

Healthcare Consumerism Matures

Patients are no longer passive recipients—they are informed, digitally fluent, and brand-sensitive. Today's healthcare consumer evaluates providers with the same scrutiny they apply to airlines, tech platforms, or retail experiences. They compare online reviews, demand cost transparency, expect real-time access, and gravitate toward brands that speak to their values.

This shift forces a profound operational transformation—from provider-centric operations to consumer-centric ecosystems. Health systems must rethink every touchpoint: appointment scheduling, digital navigation, billing clarity, communication cadence, and post-care follow-up.

Consumerism doesn't mean commoditization. It means personalization, agency, and design thinking. When a mother can book her child's pediatric visit via text, follow up with a care team through a secure app, and receive personalized health tips tied to her child's development, she doesn't just receive care—she experiences it.

Systems like One Medical, Oak Street Health, and CVS Health are setting new standards—not through clinical breakthroughs but through seamless, intuitive, human-first experiences.

And it's not just tech-savvy millennials. Seniors are adopting digital tools faster than ever. Language, accessibility, and simplicity matter deeply. Trust becomes the new brand equity.

For leaders, patient experience isn't just a marketing strategy—it's a core operational pillar. Net promoter scores, digital conversion rates, and consumer lifetime value are becoming as essential as clinical quality metrics.

But the most visionary organizations go further. They co-design services with patients, invest in empathy-based training, and create feedback loops that don't just collect data—they act on it.

Healthcare is no longer a closed system. It's a competitive marketplace of experiences. And in a future shaped by choice, the systems that win will be the ones that listen, adapt, and serve with precision and respect.

Platformization and Interoperability

The patchwork of siloed systems is giving way to platform models—interoperable ecosystems that unify EHRs, devices, applications, and analytics into seamless infrastructure. Healthcare organizations have invested in digital tools in isolation for decades, creating fragmented data environments and broken care journeys. But now, the industry is moving toward cohesive platforms that integrate data, workflows, and services in real-time.

Platformization means systems are not just technology stacks but strategic enablers. The next-generation platform is modular, cloud-native, API-driven, and intelligence-enabled. It allows data to move securely, seamlessly, and meaningfully across the care continuum.

This shift unlocks enormous value. Clinicians no longer need to toggle between multiple systems. Patients don't have to repeat their medical histories across providers. Care teams can collaborate across geography. And leaders gain access to enterprise-wide insights that fuel precision operations and system-wide learning.

Examples include platforms like Epic Cosmos, which unifies clinical research across institutions, or health systems leveraging Microsoft Cloud for Healthcare to integrate scheduling, documentation, remote monitoring, and analytics on a single spine.

Interoperability isn't just a tech problem—it's a leadership strategy. It reduces duplication, enhances safety, and improves experience. It turns data into an enterprise asset—not a byproduct.

However, it requires more than compliance with data exchange standards. True interoperability demands governance, incentives, and cultural buy-in. It means breaking down turf wars, aligning on data definitions, and investing in interfaces that respect security and usability.

To thrive in the platform era, healthcare organizations must stop seeing technology as infrastructure and treat it as architecture. Because in the future, competitive advantage won't lie in how much data you own but in how intelligently you connect, interpret, and act on it.

The Economic Rebalancing of Healthcare

Cost pressures, labor shortages, aging populations, and policy turbulence force a financial reckoning in healthcare. The old formula—more volume equals more revenue—has broken down. What remains is a race to rebalance the equation: quality, access, equity, and innovation must all improve without proportionally increasing costs.

This is not about austerity. It's about redesigning the economic architecture of healthcare.

Payers and providers alike are being pushed toward new incentives. Capitated models, bundled payments, value-based contracting, and shared-risk agreements are no longer experiments—they're becoming default arrangements in many regions. Systems that once relied heavily on fee-for-service must now prove value across episodes of care, across populations, and over time.

Vertical integration is accelerating. Health systems are acquiring physician groups, payers are becoming providers, and retailers are embedding themselves in primary care. The race is on to build end-to-end control over care delivery and cost.

However, economic sustainability also requires internal transformation. High fixed-cost structures, bloated administrative overhead, and clinical variation must be addressed through radical transparency and continuous redesign.

Systems like Intermountain and Geisinger are proving that disciplined attention to clinical pathways, predictive analytics, and utilization management can drive down costs while preserving outcomes.

And there's another layer: consumer price sensitivity is rising. Employers are shifting more costs to employees. Patients are comparing prices. Regulators are mandating transparency. Hospitals must not only compete on clinical quality but also on value propositions that resonate financially.

Workforce economics cannot be ignored. Labor makes up over 50% of healthcare spending. Burnout, attrition, and wage pressures require more imaginative workforce design—leveraging team-based models, advanced practice providers, and automation where appropriate.

Finally, economic rebalancing is about reinvestment. Systems must find ways to reduce waste, reallocate capital, and fund innovation—from home-based care to AI infrastructure.

Financial resilience won't come from being the cheapest in the next era. It will come from being the most strategic. The organizations that thrive will not be those that spend less but are more thoughtful.

The Platformization Ladder

Stages of Digital Maturity in Healthcare

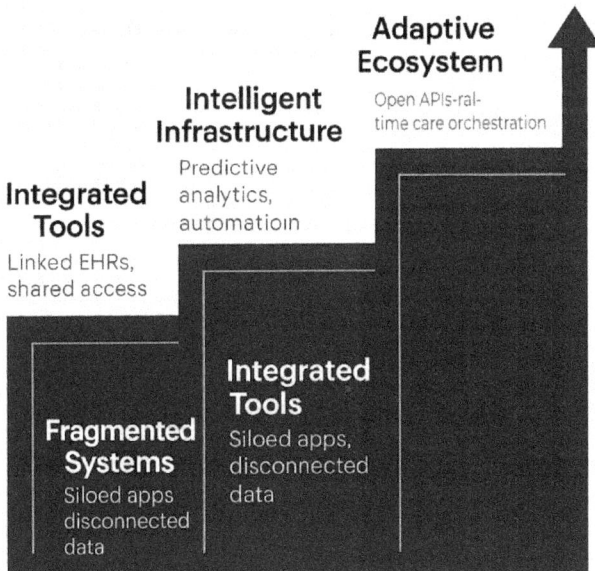

Adaptive Ecosystem
Open APIs-ral-time care orchestration

Intelligent Infrastructure
Predictive analytics, automatioın

Integrated Tools
Linked EHRs, shared access

Integrated Tools
Siloed apps, disconnected data

Fragmented Systems
Siloed apps disconnected data

The Rise of Intelligent Infrastructure

AI is no longer a futuristic concept—it's becoming embedded across clinical, operational, and administrative functions. But intelligence is not just about tools. It's about building systems that can learn, adapt, and optimize themselves in real-time. The future won't be defined by how much tech an organization buys but by how well its infrastructure can interpret signals and act on them.

Intelligent infrastructure combines advanced analytics, machine learning, real-time monitoring, and decision support into a continuous loop of learning and response. In leading systems, AI algorithms identify high-risk patients before symptoms, predict surgical complications, triage staffing shortages, and automate administrative workflows.

Consider a hospital command center powered by AI that monitors capacity, staffing, throughput, and patient acuity across departments—adjusting operations dynamically. Or an oncology platform that learns from every tumor it treats, refining protocols across a network in real-time.

Yet, building intelligence into infrastructure is not just about algorithms. It requires system-wide connectivity, cloud-first strategies, strong data governance, and digital ethics. It demands leaders who can balance innovation with trust—ensuring transparency, explainability, and accountability in AI deployment.

It also calls for operational redesign. Intelligent infrastructure requires new talent (data scientists, informaticists, and AI product managers), new workflows (integrated with clinical decision-making), and new partnerships with health tech firms.

The investment is not trivial, but the payoff is profound. Organizations that harness intelligent infrastructure can reduce variation, eliminate waste, accelerate insights, and unlock enterprise agility.

And as the pace of change accelerates, the only systems that will keep up are those that can learn faster than the world changes.

This is not about AI replacing humans. It's about AI augmenting systems so clinicians, leaders, and patients are better supported, better informed, and educated than ever before.

Workforce Reimagined

Burnout, generational shifts, and new expectations about flexibility and meaning are transforming the healthcare workforce. The pandemic didn't just strain the system—it redefined the contract between institutions and their people. Clinicians and support staff are rethinking what they want from work: a job, a sense of impact, belonging, and balance.

The future isn't just about recruitment—it's about reinvention.

That reinvention starts with well-being. Healthcare workers experience some of the highest rates of burnout, mental distress, and moral injury. Future-ready systems treat this not as an HR problem but a leadership priority. They invest in mental health support, psychological safety, trauma-informed leadership, and protected time for recovery.

Upskilling is the next frontier. With AI, telehealth, and automation transforming roles, systems must invest in continuous learning—helping staff evolve from task executors to knowledge workers, digital navigators, and care collaborators. Learning shouldn't be episodic. It should be embedded into daily practice.

Workforce models must also become more agile. Rigid hierarchies lead to team-based care, shared decision-making, and cross-functional pods. Healthcare is becoming a system of roles in flux—requiring new credentialing pathways, governance, and accountability structures, from advanced practice providers to digitally enabled support roles.

Leaders must also design for generational diversity. Younger workers prioritize flexibility, inclusion, feedback, and social impact. Legacy systems must evolve to offer career lattices, not just ladders—where talent can grow horizontally, rotationally, and experientially.

Diversity, equity, and inclusion are no longer optional. They're essential to both mission and performance. Future-ready workforces reflect their communities—not just in demographics but in lived experience and perspective. Representation must extend to leadership pipelines, boardrooms, and innovation teams.

Finally, the workforce strategy must be narrative. People don't just want to know what to do—they want to see why it matters. Purpose alignment is one of the most potent retention levers available.

Ultimately, the health systems that thrive won't be those with the most extensive recruitment budgets. They'll be the ones who design cultures where people can do their best work, bring their whole selves, and leave better than they arrived.

Closing Reflection

Megatrends aren't forecasts. They're signals—early indicators of where the tectonic plates beneath our industry are shifting. They don't just illuminate what's changing. They reveal what will be expected of leaders who hope to shape that change.

The most transformative organizations aren't waiting for complete clarity. They are prototyping new models while uncertainty still looms. They are embedding foresight into their culture—not as a one-time strategic planning exercise but as an ongoing leadership discipline.

To act on megatrends is to bet on the future—and then build systems resilient enough to adapt when the future inevitably surprises you.

This isn't about becoming futurists. It's about becoming stewards—of innovation, values, and people.

These trends don't just describe where healthcare is going—they represent the attitude of thinking the future will demand. No more meetings. More imagination. No more reports. More resolve.

Visionary leaders won't just respond to the moment. They'll redesign the future it leads to. They'll interpret signals. They'll make bets. And they'll build cultures capable of growing forward, not just old.

"See the trends, make bold bends. Lead the change that never ends."

— **Sumit Sharma**

Section 2: Scenario Planning – What Will 2045 Look Like?

Futures-Based Planning Grid
Strategic Responses to Four Possible Futures

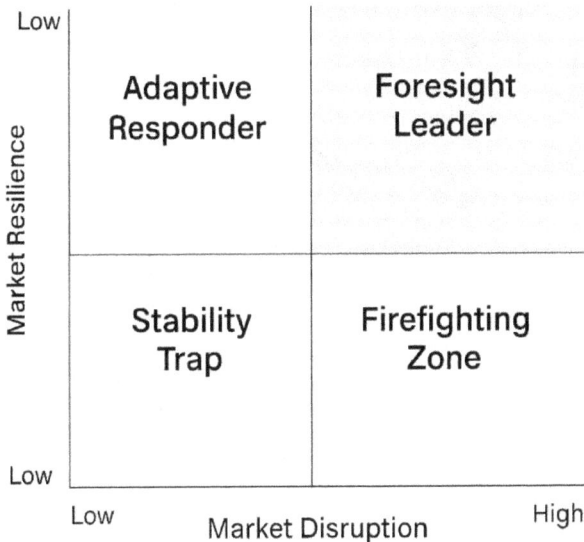

	Low	
Market Resilience	Adaptive Responder	Foresight Leader
	Stability Trap	Firefighting Zone
Low		
	Low Market Disruption High	

If a leader today walked into a boardroom and predicted that by 2045, 80% of care would be delivered at home, organs would be bio-printed on demand, and every patient would have a personal AI care advisor—they might be dismissed as overly imaginative. But history has always been built by those who dared to imagine.

Scenario planning is not about predicting one outcome. It's about preparing for multiple plausible futures. It's a strategic discipline that allows leaders to navigate uncertainty—not with rigid forecasts but with adaptable vision. The question is not "What will happen?" but "What could happen, and how do we lead through it?"

This section paints vivid pictures of the healthcare landscape in 2045—based on current signals, emerging technologies, policy trajectories, demographic realities, and behavioral shifts. From personalized health ecosystems and AI-native health systems to climate-adaptive hospitals and regenerative medicine breakthroughs, we explore the contours of tomorrow's care—and the leadership it will demand.

This is not fiction. It is disciplined foresight because the leaders who can visualize the horizon are the ones who will be trusted to build toward it.

Let us now step twenty years forward—to a time where today's strategies will either look prophetic or obsolete—and ask: What kind of world are we building, and who will be bold enough to lead it?

Scenario 1: Mary's Journey — Living Through a GI Cancer in 2045

Mary was 52 when her care journey began. She wasn't expecting anything unusual that morning in the spring of 2045. A gentle vibration from her bathroom mirror—a part of her home's ambient health monitoring system— alerted her to a subtle shift. Her latest digestive biomarkers, monitored through continuous noninvasive sensors embedded in her toilet and toothbrush, showed a pattern that deviated from her baseline. Nothing urgent. But worth reviewing.

Within 30 seconds, her AI companion—Aria—offered a calm suggestion: "Mary, I've flagged a gastrointestinal pattern I'd like our physician partner to review. Can we schedule a remote exam this morning?"

By noon, Mary was on a video call—not with a single provider, but with a precision care pod: a generalist, a GI specialist, and an AI clinician working together on a dynamic screen. All of them were looking at the same real-time diagnostic dashboard, which had already run predictive models based on Mary's genetic risk, epigenetic drift, microbiome trends, social determinants, and longitudinal health history.

The model showed a 76% probability of early-stage colorectal cancer. Aria had already scheduled a same-day AI-navigated capsule endoscopy—a swallowable, camera-equipped smart pill—delivered by drone to Mary's home. She took it with a glass of water that evening.

A System That Knows and Shows Up

By the following day, Mary's results had been analyzed. AI-enhanced high-resolution 4D imaging, identified a suspicious lesion. A collaborative tumor board convened—remotely within hours. The board included human clinicians, digital oncologists, molecular surgeons, and an ethicist.

Unlike the fragmented experience of 2024, Mary didn't have to make multiple appointments, repeat her history a dozen times, or hand-carry imaging results. Her data flowed seamlessly, securely, and intelligently—across systems, specialties, and time. The infrastructure had absorbed the burden of coordination, once hers to carry.

Her entire tumor genome was sequenced within 45 minutes from a cheek swab. No authorizations. No insurance pre-calls. Payment models had evolved: Mary's care was automatically pre-approved through a value-based national health plan that aligned incentives with outcomes—not billing codes.

Bloodwork? Already done. Her intelligent countertop device had tested everything from CBC to metabolic panels through a fingertip scan while she made tea the day before.

Her treatment plan? Completely customized: a minimally invasive surgical intervention to remove the tumor, followed by targeted cellular immunotherapy tailored to her exact mutational profile.

No waiting. No redundancy. No fear of being lost in the system.

Aria explained everything in clear, calm language. It was not a script, but a personalized conversation adjusted to Mary's tone, pacing, and emotional state. "Mary," she said, "the good news is: we found it early. And you are not alone."

Surgery, But Not as We Know It

Three days later, Mary's front door opened to a compact autonomous surgical unit—delivered by an accredited mobile hospital service. This wasn't a tech gimmick. It was a fully licensed, AI-powered microsurgical suite capable of performing complex procedures once reserved for operating rooms of elite academic hospitals. The shift wasn't just in location—inexperience, control, and human dignity.

Her home had already been scanned and prepared. Environmental sensors recalibrated humidity, filtration, sound, and temperature. A sterilization drone had mapped the surgical zone. A diagnostic avatar walked Mary through the final pre-op steps, not with cold, clinical language but in the warm voice of someone who understood her preferences, her anxiety, and her curiosity.

The procedure was performed by a globally ranked GI surgeon—connected from Singapore—and supported by haptic AI arms locally housed in the surgical pod. Machine vision ensured sub-millimeter precision. The AI system adjusted every movement in real-time, integrating Mary's vitals, prior imaging, and anatomical variation.

A biometric feedback loop adjusted anesthesia dosage dynamically, avoiding the fog and nausea she remembered from her mother's hospital surgeries.

She wasn't alone. Her son sat beside her. Her care dog rested nearby. She watched a projected sky on the ceiling that mimicked the view from a mountain cabin they once visited together. The technology faded into the background—what remained was safety, stillness, and control.

During post-op recovery, her room's AI recalibrated lighting based on cortisol levels delivered hydration prompts based on hydration biomarkers, and adjusted her personalized nutrition plan. There was no nurse call button. The room anticipated her needs.

She drifted into post-op rest, not under harsh fluorescent lights but under the soft skylight of her ceiling, surrounded by the warmth of her life—not the sterility of a ward.

Recovery, Reimagined

Over the next six weeks, Mary's immunotherapy was delivered via personalized bio-nanoparticles, calibrated in real-time based on her cytokine response and metabolic variability. The precision was astounding—her dosages adjusted not weekly but hourly in response to real-time data. She never had to visit a pharmacy. Every dose arrived through an automated delivery pod, coordinated by her intelligent care OS, and verified through her biometric scan.

No paperwork. No prior authorizations. There are no pharmacy queues. Everything that used to steal her time, her peace of mind, and her dignity had quietly disappeared into the background.

Her emotional health was treated as non-negotiable. She wasn't simply prescribed rest—she was surrounded by support. Her AI therapist, trained in oncology care and adaptive counseling techniques, checked in daily—adjusting her tone and approach based on her vocal stress patterns. A rotating circle of peer support avatars, modeled after real cancer survivors who had volunteered to share their stories, kept her connected to meaning.

Even her physical therapy was no longer a lonely experience. Each morning, she entered a mixed-reality forest—its terrain customized to her rehabilitation needs. Her movements were captured through wearable motion sensors that transmitted progress to her care team, who reviewed them asynchronously and adjusted her exercises weekly.

Meal planning and nutrition—once a guessing game— were curated based on Mary's metabolic needs, taste preferences, and cultural identity. She even received morning "micro-cooking" tutorials for immune-boosting meals she could prepare in five minutes.

Every aspect of Mary's journey—from diagnosis to remission—was powered by a system that didn't just treat the disease. It saw her. It listened. It stayed ahead of her needs. It gave her back time, trust, and control.

She didn't just survive cancer. She healed as a whole person, supported by a system finally designed around her life—not its limitations.

What This Scenario Tells Us

This isn't just about futuristic tech. It's about rethinking the entire architecture of care—through the eyes of the patient.

Mary's story reminds us of all the invisible burdens people carry in today's system: navigating appointments, re-explaining symptoms, reconciling bills, chasing referrals, waiting for imaging, advocating for themselves across specialties, and wondering if anyone is steering the ship. Those burdens didn't come from the disease. They came from the system.

But in Mary's world, they're gone. Not because they were ignored—but because they were designed out.

- Proactive discovery replaces episodic detection.
- Personalized precision replaces protocol-driven plans.
- Home-based, system-enabled delivery replaces hospital dependence.
- Emotionally intelligent support replaces fragmented follow-up.
- Embedded coordination replaces patient-led navigation.
- Outcome-driven payment replaces billing-based delay.

Mary's story is a window into a system where care moves at the speed of trust, data serves dignity, and technology is invisible—yet indispensable. It's not science fiction. It's strategic design.

The future doesn't arrive all at once. It's built, piece by piece, by leaders bold enough to imagine it—and practical sufficient to operationalize it.

If we want care to be humane, accessible, and wise in 2045—we must stop optimizing around what care was and start building what care could be.

That future is not someone else's responsibility. It's ours.

"Build for the human, not just the outcome. Design for the life, not just the disease."

— **Sumit Sharma**

Scenario 2: Aidan's Arc — Adolescent Mental Health in a World That Finally Listens

Aidan was 16 when the silence stopped being safe. His grades had dropped, his sleep was fractured, and his search history revealed more about his loneliness than he could say aloud. In 2024, he might've gone unnoticed—or worse, been misdiagnosed and brushed aside by a system too overwhelmed to care.

But in 2045, the system doesn't wait for the child to speak. It listens—quietly, respectfully, continuously.

Aidan's AI-enabled learning pod had already picked up subtle signals: diminished engagement, vocal tone changes, and delayed reactions in collaborative games. Combined with biometric sleep irregularities and reduced physical activity flagged by his wearable, his care OS sensed a deviation from the baseline.

Rather than trigger alarms or shame, it initiated care through invitation. His AI school counselor avatar appeared during study hall—not as a disciplinary presence, but as a curious, caring peer. "Hey, Aidan. You've been quiet lately. Want to check in?"

Within hours, his parents were privately looped in. His trusted family physician—who'd followed Aidan's care journey from childhood—joined a virtual support circle alongside a licensed adolescent therapist and an AI mental health guide trained in generational communication and trauma-informed care.

There were no referrals to chase. No insurance denials. No 3-month waitlists. The system moved at the speed of emotional need.

Care That Feels Like Belonging

Aidan was never handed a clipboard. He wasn't ushered into a cold clinic room or asked to relieve pain in front of strangers. Instead, his care unfolded naturally— like a thoughtful conversation across time.

His virtual therapist avatar, modeled after a young mentor he once admired, built rapport gradually. They played strategy games, shared music, and talked casually— layer by layer, trust forming like sediment. Beneath the surface, the avatar's neural engine tracked stress markers, linguistic patterns, and emotional responsiveness to guide clinical insight without pressure.

Aidan's treatment wasn't protocol—it was orchestration. He was offered a menu of support pathways, from group VR therapy with peers across the globe to somatic release movement guided by haptic feedback to private narrative journaling analyzed gently for trauma markers.

His family received an education—not judgment. Parents were supported with behavioral nudges, contextual coaching, and reminders that healing didn't come from control but from connection. His care team used a shared emotional graph to track relational dynamics over time, adjusting support levels not based on incident but trajectory.

Everything was integrated: sleep restoration via circadian lighting, microdosing therapies monitored through breath analytics, AI cognitive coaching for executive function, and music-driven neuroplasticity tools personalized to Aidan's neural rhythm.

There was no "mental health crisis." There was just life—with its highs, lows, and complexity—met by a system that could hold it without collapsing.

Healing, Not Just Coping

Aidan didn't need to be fixed. He needed to be witnessed, heard, and empowered. He needed a system that didn't pathologize emotion or medicalize identity but reflected his capacity to heal, grow, and lead.

In the old system, he might've been hospitalized, medicated without context, or pushed into cookie-cutter solutions that treated symptoms but missed the story. In 2045, the system saw his wholeness before it saw his diagnosis.

He co-authored his recovery journey. He painted murals that expressed grief and hope. He composed music in his neurofeedback studio, where each note helped him regulate mood through bio-responsive rhythm. He engaged in immersive story circles—virtual campfires where teens shared not advice but presence.

His re-entry into school was not marked by paperwork or labels but by a portfolio of strengths—emotional intelligence badges, resilience micro-credentials, and a personal narrative that showcased who he was becoming.

His healing team extended beyond therapists. It included community elders, peer guides, AI companions who translated stress into strategy, and a teacher who incorporated mental wellness into the curriculum—not as a module but as a muscle.

Every step was logged, not in a cold, clinical chart but in a beautifully designed life journey map. It wasn't about compliance. It was about coherence.

He didn't just bounce back—he bounced forward, carrying tools, insights, and relationships that formed the foundation of a lifelong emotional architecture.

Healing wasn't a detour. It was the main path. And in a world that honored that truth, Aidan didn't just find his footing—he found his voice.

What This Scenario Tells Us

Mental health systems in 2045 don't wait for a breakdown. They are built upstream, with the architecture of listening, empathy, and adaptability embedded into daily life. They shift from episodic intervention to relational constancy—tuning in before tuning out becomes a crisis.

Aidan's story is more than a patient vignette—it refines how systems can operate when they start from trust rather than thresholds. It shows us what happens when care design is no longer reactive but predictive, ambient, and deeply human.

His journey proves that agency and support are not opposites but partners. He wasn't given a diagnosis and was discharged. He was invited into a process where healing became identity-building, not symptom suppression.

It reminds us that dignity in mental health isn't about protecting from shame. It's about eliminating the conditions that create it. It's about designing systems so humane, integrated, and anticipatory that shame never has to exist in the first place.

In this future, emotional pain is not a signal of failure. It is treated as a natural part of being alive, deserving of curiosity, community, and care.

The lesson is simple yet radical: the more our systems learn to listen, the fewer people will feel the need to scream to be heard.

"We don't heal by fixing minds. We heal by building systems that never forget the heart."

— **Sumit Sharma**

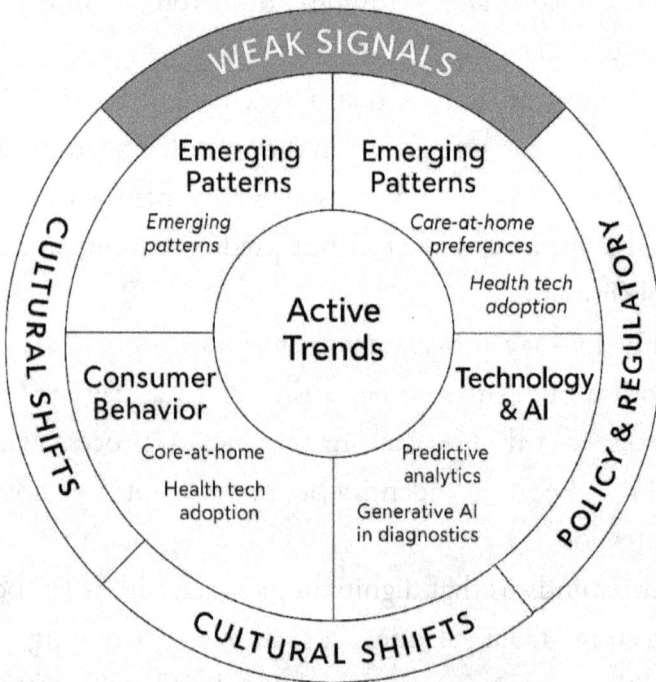

Section 3: Strategic Visioning in an Uncertain World

Healthcare is not just in transition—it's in transformation. The difference is essential. Transition implies movement between known points. Transformation, on the other hand, means crossing into territory that has no map.

In this environment, traditional planning frameworks fall short. They are built on assumptions of linear change, stable variables, and gradual evolution. However, strategic clarity must come from a different place in a world defined by exponential technologies, demographic inversion, geopolitical volatility, and climate disruption.

That place is vision. Not as a poster slogan or a five-year goal—but as a disciplined capacity to imagine, synthesize, and align toward futures that don't yet exist.

Strategic visioning in healthcare is about scanning signals, naming tensions, and creating architectures of optionality. It means leading systems not with perfect forecasts but with flexible intent. It means building organizations that can move with conviction even when uncertain.

This section unpacks how leaders can cultivate that vision—not as an inherited trait but as a teachable, practicable skill. Because the future will not reward perfection, it will reward coherence, courage, and the ability to adapt at the speed of relevance.

We'll explore tools, postures, and mindsets that enable organizations to look beyond next quarter's metrics and toward the next decade's legacy. In an age of intelligent machines and uncertain outcomes, it is not the most innovative system that survives. It has the most straightforward direction, deepest values, and incredible ability to act before consensus.

From Forecasting to Foresight

Forecasting is about predicting what will happen. Foresight is about preparing for what could happen.

Most healthcare organizations still operate in a forecasting mindset: they project trends based on past performance, run static financial models, and assume the continuity of variables. But as the last decade has shown—from pandemics to AI acceleration to workforce disruption—the future is rarely linear and seldom polite enough to fit into a spreadsheet.

Foresight begins by accepting ambiguity. It embraces weak signals, emerging patterns, and radical possibilities. It asks, "what is likely?" but also "what is plausible, what is possible, and what is preferred?"

A foresight mindset encourages scenario thinking, horizon scanning, and creative tension. It's less about answers and more about questions:

- What are the edge signals we are ignoring?
- Where are our assumptions vulnerable?

- What blind spots could disrupt our current strategy?
- How would we act differently if we knew a significant shift was 24 months away?

However, foresight is not an abstract exercise; it must be embedded into organizational discipline. It requires time on senior leadership agendas, structured scanning rituals, and diverse teams empowered to challenge orthodoxy. It rewards leaders who can sit with uncertainty long enough to see what others rush to simplify.

Healthcare systems with strong foresight capabilities develop what military strategists call "strategic elasticity"—the ability to hold a clear direction while adapting tactics to shifting ground. They prototype early, adjust quickly, and avoid over-committing to brittle strategies.

Examples are emerging: systems designing climate-resilient campuses in response to early environmental signals—pediatric hospitals planning for demographic collapse. Integrated care organizations are designing AI-augmented clinical workflows—not because it's urgent now but because it will be inevitable soon.

Foresight doesn't predict the future. It prepares you to shape it.

Leaders who develop foresight capacity learn to distinguish between noise and signal, urgency and importance, and trends and truths. They don't just react to disruption. They pre-position their organizations to absorb it, learn from it, and sometimes—lead it.

In healthcare, where lagging indicators often dominate, foresight creates a way to lead with anticipation instead of explanation. That shift may be a leader's most strategic move in a world where relevance is perishable.

Signal Scanning and Strategic Imagination

Strategic vision doesn't start with answers—it begins with curiosity. Leaders who want to shape the future must become disciplined observers of the present. Signal scanning detects faint pulses from the future embedded in today's noise.

These signals don't always appear in peer-reviewed journals or government white papers. They emerge in unlikely places: startup pitches, art exhibits, science fiction, social media behaviors, supply chain anomalies, or shifts in how teenagers use language. Each may seem trivial in isolation. But viewed together, they form a constellation.

Healthcare leaders must develop a wide-angle vision to spot clinical trends and cultural undercurrents. Not just economic models but human behaviors. Not just technologies but shifts in trust, values, and time horizons.

But scanning alone is not enough. Strategic imagination is what connects the dots. It's the ability to leap from signal to possibility, trend to implication, and from to design. It allows a CEO to say, "If this continues, what does our system look like in 2045?" or "If this breaks, what new value might emerge?"

Organizations that make room for imagination don't just read signals—they rehearse futures. They host foresight workshops, conduct speculative design sprints, and create shadow boards with younger staff. They embed storytellers alongside analysts. They invite outlier perspectives—not to disrupt but to stretch.

Strategic imagination isn't about blue-sky dreaming. It's about generating practical hypotheses that allow systems to test new pathways before they're forced to.

The most visionary health systems don't just scale what works today. They also invest in what might matter tomorrow—long before the ROI is clear.

In a field trained to minimize risk, strategic imagination reminds us that the most considerable risk may be playing it too safe.

Optionality as a Design Principle

In a world where linear plans fail fast, resilient systems are not built on certainty but on optionality.

Optionality is the ability to pursue multiple paths, experiment with parallel ideas, and course-correct without collapse. It is not indecision. It is strategic flexibility baked into the design.

For too long, healthcare systems have been rewarded for commitment to a singular EHR, a flagship building, or a specific care model. But in an age of volatility, commitment without optionality becomes fragile.

Leading organizations now architect their strategies to include room for divergence. They build modular technology stacks that allow future integration. They pilot multiple staffing models. They invest in adjacent markets. They develop strategic "off-ramps" and "on-ramps" for innovation partnerships. They scale in ways that preserve maneuverability.

Optionality is not inefficient. It's a hedge against irrelevance.

Consider it as holding strategic inventory—not of materials, but of ideas, relationships, and pilot programs ready to expand or exit, depending on the scenario. It's the equivalent of having more than one door out of the room.

Healthcare's most resilient systems do not have the most detailed 10-year plans. They have the most viable options—well-developed, tested, and ready to activate when the winds change.

Strategic visioning in uncertainty means designing for resilience without rigidity. Optionality is how you honor the unknown without being paralyzed by it.

Leading with Coherence in a Fragmented Age

In the noise of transformation, coherence becomes a superpower. While disruption celebrates novelty and agility, emphasizing speed, coherence is the quiet force that makes all movement meaningful.

Coherence doesn't mean conformity. It means alignment—between values and actions, vision and execution, short-term pressures, and long-term purpose. In healthcare, coherence is what prevents strategic whiplash. It ensures that innovation doesn't become a series of disconnected bets but instead ladders up to a straightforward and courageous narrative.

In a fragmented environment—where systems are stretched across locations, technologies, partnerships, and care models—coherence is what binds identity. It allows a rural hospital and an urban flagship to operate with shared DNA. It's what makes a frontline nurse, a CFO, and a tech strategist feel like they're building the same future.

To lead with coherence, organizations must:

- Anchor decisions on purpose, not just performance.
- Design incentives that align behaviors across functions.
- Communicate vision repeatedly, in multiple modalities, until it becomes culture.
- Declutter governance to reduce friction and enhance clarity.
- Use narrative not just as PR but as operating logic.

When coherence is strong, teams move faster—not because they're micromanaged but because the path is visible. They know where they're going, why it matters, and how they can contribute.

Visionary leaders don't just chase transformation. They curate coherence. They help people make sense of change, stay rooted in meaning, and act with integrity across uncertainty.

In the end, transformation without coherence is just chaos in disguise.

Closing Reflection

Vision is not a luxury—it's a lifeline. In an industry built on tradition, regulation, and risk aversion, strategic visioning pulls organizations out of maintenance mode and into momentum.

The future is not just uncertain—it's nonlinear, fast-moving, and discontinuous. What separates resilient systems from obsolete ones is not how quickly they react but how they see—before others do.

This chapter is not a call to predict everything. Imagining boldly, preparing generously, and acting more coherently is a challenge. The leaders who thrive in uncertainty do not have the perfect plan. They have the most apparent purpose and the most expansive field of view.

They don't chase every trend—they connect the right ones.

They don't rely on hope—they design for optionality.

And above all, they don't just adapt to the future—they help shape it.

"Don't wait for certainty to lead. Build the map as you walk the terrain."

— **Sumit Sharma**

Readiness for Transformation Grid

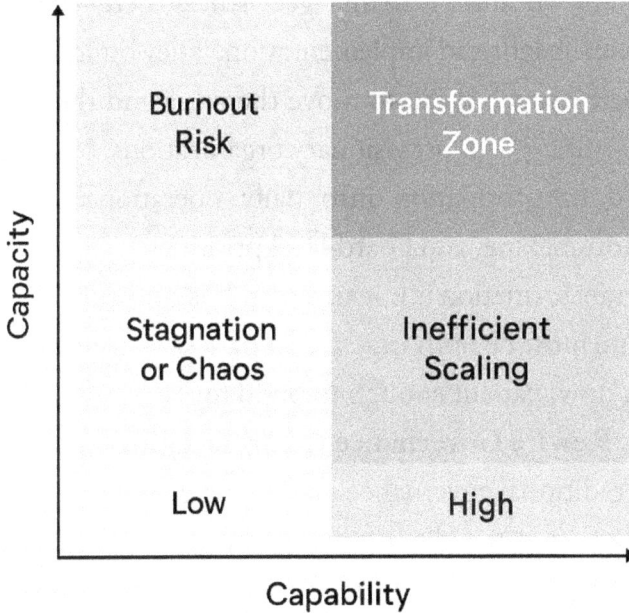

© 2025 Sharmx Leadership LLC. All rights reserved

Section 4: From Trends to Transformation – What Leaders Must Do Now

Knowing the trends is not enough. Leaders' real challenge—and opportunity—is translating foresight into action. While scenario planning helps envision the future, it is only as valuable as the choices it influences, the resources it reallocates, and the courage it builds.

Trends tell us where things are headed. Transformation asks: What will we do differently now that we know?

Many health systems get stuck here—paralyzed between insight and implementation. They build beautiful strategic plans but fail to move them beyond the walls of the C-suite. The most visionary organizations, by contrast, embed transformation into daily operations, frontline decision-making, and board-level priorities.

Transformation is not an event. It is a posture. And the posture must be both urgent and patient—urgent enough to act now, patient enough to build for later.

1. Rewire Governance to Drive Agility

Traditional governance models were built for scale and stability—not speed and sense-making. Committees meet quarterly. Approvals cascade slowly. Strategic pivots must pass through bottlenecks. In today's volatile world, that model has become a liability.

Agile governance redefines decision rights: who decides, how fast, and with what level of fidelity. It empowers cross-functional teams to prototype and iterate. It builds transparency through open dashboards, real-time insights, and shared accountability.

This isn't about eliminating structure—it's about updating it. Board charters should include innovation KPIs. Executive teams should review not just financial performance but transformation velocity. Agility is not chaos. It's coherence in motion.

2. Fund Futures, Not Just Fixes

Most budgets are built backward, starting from last year's numbers, adding incremental changes, and protecting legacy programs. However, transformation requires investment in possibility, not just repair.

Forward-looking systems create "futures funds"— protected capital for new models, long bets, and adaptive strategies. They track ROI in dollars and insight gained, capabilities developed, and risk de-risked.

They also reward learning. Failed pilots are not punished—they are mined for intelligence because a dollar spent on learning now is worth ten in crisis response later.

3. Lead with Narratives, Not Just Numbers

We live in an era of information fatigue. What breaks through is not more data—it's better stories. Numbers can inform, but stories inspire.

To drive transformation, leaders must become chief meaning officers. They must communicate what is changing and why it matters to clinicians, staff, and staff. They must craft strategic narratives that link head and heart, strategy and soul.

The narrative is not fluff—it's infrastructure. When done well, it aligns teams, reduces resistance, and accelerates adoption. It turns change from a threat into a shared journey.

4. Build Capability for Change, Not Just Capacity

Health systems often confuse scale with readiness. But adding more people or more tools doesn't guarantee transformation. What matters more is capability—the skills, mindsets, and fluency to operate in complexity.

Future-ready organizations invest in:

- Strategic foresight as a leadership skill.
- Systems thinking for complex problem-solving.
- Human-centered design to create with, not for, communities.
- Digital fluency at every level—not just in IT departments.

They treat learning not as episodic but as ambient. They build cultures where inquiry is celebrated, reflection is routine, and experimentation is safe.

5. Make Transformation Everyone's Job

Transformation fails when it's confined to silos. Real change becomes possible only when everyone—from the frontline nurse to the facilities engineer to the patient family advisor—has a role.

This means a democratizing strategy. It means co-designing solutions with end users. It means surfacing ideas from the edges of the organization, not just the center.

It also means aligning incentives. If transformation is genuinely strategic, performance reviews, promotion pathways, and recognition programs should reflect it.

When a transformation is shared, it becomes sustainable. When it is owned across layers, it moves faster and sticks longer.

The path from trends to transformation is not linear. But it is navigable—for those willing to act before they are confident, include voices beyond their own, and invest in tomorrow as urgently as they manage today.

Because in healthcare, the most dangerous myth is that the future is someone else's job.

"Transformation doesn't begin with technology or trend reports. It begins when leadership becomes a verb."

— **Sumit Sharma**

Section 5: The Stewardship Mindset – Leading for the Long Game

Healthcare leadership has traditionally been measured by how well one delivers in the short term—budgets balanced, initiatives launched, metrics met. But the future will increasingly belong to those who think like stewards, not just strategists.

Stewardship is about planting trees under whose shade you may never sit. It's about holding the organization in trust—not just for shareholders or stakeholders today, but for generations of patients, communities, and caregivers tomorrow.

In this final section of Chapter 8, we explore what it means to lead with the long game in mind—why stewardship is not a soft skill but a strategic imperative. We'll dive into how systems can embed sustainability, intergenerational thinking, equity, and ethical design into the core of their strategic playbook.

Visionaries don't just navigate change; they cultivate legacy.

"A leader's true impact is measured not by what they control, but by what they leave behind." — Sumit Sharma

Legacy Thinking in a Quarterly World

Clocks surround today's health systems. Quarterly earnings, fiscal targets, performance dashboards, and short-cycle KPIs dominate leadership attention. And yet, most of the challenges that matter—climate resilience, community trust, chronic disease reduction, generational trauma—unfold on timelines that defy these rhythms.

Legacy thinking is looking beyond the immediate to steward the durable. It is not about abandoning accountability. It is about redefining what we are accountable to.

Steward leaders don't just ask, "What will this quarter show?" They ask, "How will this decision echo 10 years from now?"

They plant programs, policies, and principles that may take decades to mature:

- Investing in the health of toddlers to reduce ICU admissions 20 years later.
- Decarbonizing infrastructure today to serve communities in a hotter world.
- Building clinician pipeline partnerships in underserved areas for 2040 staffing.
- Designing AI governance that prioritizes human dignity for generations.

Legacy thinking requires resisting urgency bias. It requires courage to defend the unmeasurable and advocate for the unborn.

And it's not theoretical. Health systems with long-term logic often outperform trust, loyalty, and resilience—especially during crises. Because when a community believes your commitment is generational, not transactional, they stay with you.

Legacy is not what you say you stand for. Others carry it forward when you're no longer in the room.

The long game is not a luxury—it's leadership's most sacred responsibility.

Enterprise Stewardship: Securing Value Across Generations

In large health systems, scale amplifies both potential and risk. A single strategic misstep can ripple across millions of lives, hundreds of communities, and billions in public trust. That's why stewardship, at the enterprise level, is more than an ethical stance—it's a strategic necessity.

Enterprise stewardship begins by recognizing that sustainability, equity, and intergenerational impact are not adjacent to value—they are valued.

A system's true worth is measured not just in EBITDA or market share but in its resilience across generations, trust equity with communities, and capacity to adapt without abandoning identity.

CEOs and boards who adopt a stewardship mindset embed it across five enterprise domains:

1. Strategic Investments with a Long Horizon
   - Shift capital allocation toward multi-decade infrastructure—green campuses, digital equity initiatives, and long-view workforce pipelines.

- Avoid short-term returns that mortgage the system's future capacity.

2. Governance That Transcends the Tenure Clock
   - Build governance models that institutionalize stewardship beyond the CEO's term—embedding long-range metrics into board oversight and incentive structures.

3. Trust as an Asset Class
   - Trust should not be treated as a soft virtue but a hard asset. Monitor, measure, and grow it across patient populations, employee cohorts, and the broader public.
   - Stewardship leaders understand that trust compounds when earned but collapses fast when neglected.

4. Ethical Design in Innovation
   - Use foresight to ensure emerging technologies—especially AI, genomics, and automation—are implemented with dignity, equity, and long-term governance in place.

5. Workforce Sustainability as Enterprise Strategy
   - Embed well-being, flexible careers, and meaning-making into the DNA of organizational design—not as HR perks, but as a core business strategy to preserve talent and institutional wisdom.

THE ENTERPRISE STEWARDSHIP MODEL
Five Pillars of Generational Healthcare Leadership

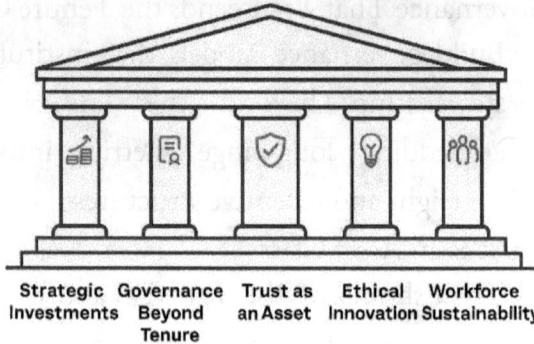

| Strategic Investments | Governance Beyond Tenure | Trust as an Asset | Ethical Innovation | Workforce Sustainability |

The most competitive systems of the future will be those seen not as extractive enterprises but as regenerative institutions—able to grow value while also growing trust, health, and hope.

Stewardship isn't just about legacy. It's about safeguarding enterprise vitality in a future that will reward those who build beyond their reflection.

Closing Reflection

Leadership in the next era will be judged not by how quickly it responded to change but by how intentionally it shaped what came next. Stewardship is not about being passive caretakers—it's about being visionary builders of durable systems that outlast our tenure and serve the public good.

To lead for the long game is to resist the gravitational pull of short-term wins and instead aim for compounding impact. It's choosing the more challenging path of discipline over the easier reaction route.

Ultimately, it anchors every decision to a more profound question: What will the next generation say we stood for?

"Legacy isn't built at the end of a career—it's shaped by every choice we make in the middle of uncertainty."

— Sumit Sharma

Chapter 9: The Visionary Leader's Playbook

There comes a point in every transformation journey when the frameworks are exhausted, the data is inconclusive, and the familiar roads have ended. What remains is the leader—alone with their values, their courage, and their capacity to choose what comes next.

This is the moment for visionary leadership.

If this book has asked one thing of you, it is this: don't just manage the future—shape it.

Visionary leadership in healthcare is not about charisma or titles. It's about courage, coherence, and the consistent ability to hold a long-term vision while navigating short-term pressures. It's the difference between leading an organization and shaping a generation.

This final chapter distills the patterns, postures, and principles that define visionary healthcare leaders. It is not a checklist. It is a compass—meant to orient your thinking, not prescribe your steps.

Because in a world where systems are strained, innovation is fragmented, and trust is eroding, the leader who can unify teams, frame complexity, and act with disciplined boldness will not just survive. They will define what healthcare becomes next.

"In times of change, the clearest vision is not held by the loudest voice—but by the leader who sees farther, listens deeper, and builds wider."

— Sumit Sharma

Vision Crafting as an Ongoing Practice

Vision is not a one-time statement—it's a living, evolving force. Previously, strategic vision was often written at offsites, polished into a slide, and referenced during annual reports. However, for the visionary leader, vision is not a static phrase. It's a muscle. And like any muscle, it requires constant engagement.

Vision must adapt without losing its center in vision must adapt without losing its center. That means continually scanning the environment, listening to the margins, and translating those signals into strategic direction.

Visionary leaders often revisit and refine their vision—not because they are unsure, but because they are paying attention. They craft vision the way an artist works a canvas: layer by layer, with room for surprises and emotional truth.

This kind of visioning work involves:

- Tethering to Purpose
  - o Vision without purpose is directionless. Leaders return to their organization's core reason for being—not as nostalgia but as fuel.
- Stretching to the Horizon
  - o They imagine a bold future. Not just what is probable but what is preferable. And they permit others to dream alongside them.
- Inviting Many Voices
  - o Vision crafted in isolation is fragile. True visionaries invite team members, patients, partners, and even critics into the process— knowing that shared ownership builds staying power.
- Making Vision Usable
  - o They translate grand ideals into usable strategic language: a vision that can guide hiring, budget allocation, clinical models, and daily decisions.

Most importantly, they never stop crafting. They are humble enough to revise and clear-eyed sufficient to recommit. They know the work is never finished because the future is constantly unfolding.

Leading Through Ambiguity

Visionary leadership begins where certainty ends. In a world of constant transformation—AI adoption, staffing volatility, climate crises, and generational divides—there is no playbook, only posture.

To lead through ambiguity is not to eliminate it but to move forward despite it. Visionary leaders do not wait for perfect information. They make meaning from the available data while acknowledging what they don't yet know.

This kind of leadership demands three things:

- Comfort with Complexity
  - o Visionaries do not simplify the world to make themselves feel in control. They hold space for contradiction. They can say, "We're doing well, and we must do better."
  - o They understand that ambiguity is not the enemy—it's the context. And their role is to make sense of it, not erase it.
- Decision-Making Under Uncertainty
  - o Visionary leaders learn how to decide without delay. They use principles, values, and directional clarity as decision scaffolds.
  - o They act, reflect, learn, and iterate—turning uncertainty into forward motion rather than analysis paralysis.

- Emotional Range and Presence
  - o Ambiguity breeds anxiety. Visionaries don't ignore that—they hold it. They offer calm in the storm without pretending to have all the answers.
  - o They normalize fear while modeling resilience. They help their teams stay grounded by radiating both empathy and resolve.

Most importantly, visionary leaders don't fake certainty. They offer something more powerful: belief. Not naive optimism but grounded conviction that we can navigate forward—together.

They turn ambiguity into alignment, not by removing complexity, but by building clarity inside it.

In uncertain times, the leader who can say, "Follow me—we won't have every answer, but we have a direction," is the one others trust most.

Building Coalitions of the Willing

No visionary leads alone. In every great transformation, from medical revolutions to operational overhauls, the actual force is not the solo genius—it's the collective momentum of people who choose to move before the path is clear.

Coalitions of the willing are made up of those who may not hold formal authority but possess deep convictions. They are nurses who pilot new workflows, analysts who reimagine data storytelling, physicians who advocate for equity-driven care models, and administrators who rewire outdated processes.

These are not just volunteers—they are architects of the future. And their power lies in their commitment, not their job titles.

The visionary leader doesn't mandate alignment. They cultivate it. They don't command buy-in—they create belonging. And in doing so, they accelerate change from the bottom up, sideways, and diagonally—because true transformation is never linear.

Naming the Why

People move toward meaning. Leaders make the purpose of change undeniable, specific, and emotionally resonant.

They don't just say what's changing—they make the cost of inaction visible by:

- Elevating the Early Movers
  - o Change spreads through the story. Visionaries spotlight early adopters—not just for outcomes, but for courage.
  - o They narrate wins, even small ones, in ways that invite replication and pride.
- Creating Low-Barrier Onramps
  - o Not everyone can leap. But many will step in if the first step feels possible. Great leaders design entry points for diverse contributors.

- o These might be pilot programs, learning labs, or open forums that allow hesitant supporters to build confidence.
- Protecting the Bold
  - o Every coalition needs air cover. Visionaries use their political capital to shield risk-takers so they can keep moving.
  - o When experiments fail—and some will— leaders frame the failure as learning, not liability.
- Letting Energy Lead
  - o Coalitions aren't always clean or linear. Leaders follow where momentum is building and support what is working.
  - o They resist the urge to control the change and instead serve as its catalyst and connector.

Most importantly, visionary leaders recognize that influence outpaces hierarchy. They pay attention to who is trusted—not just who is titled.

When people feel ownership, they are part of shaping the solution rather than just receiving the mandate, and they bring their full creativity, heart, and insight to the table.

Coalitions are powerful not because they are perfect but because they are alive. They give transformation a human engine.

In complex systems, people don't follow titles. They follow trust. And when visionary leaders build coalitions around a shared purpose, they unlock capacity beyond any org chart.

Because movements begin not with mandates—but with those who say, "I see what you see—and I'm ready to help build it."

The Courage to Act Before Consensus

Visionary leaders rarely begin with majority support. They start with conviction. They act not because the path is clear but because the direction is right.

In large systems—especially in healthcare—there is a gravitational pull toward consensus. We are waiting for alignment. We study until certainty. We delay until no one can disagree. But transformation doesn't work that way.

If you wait for everyone to agree, the moment will pass.

Visionary leadership means stepping forward before the crowd catches up. Not recklessly, but responsibly grounded in values, informed by strategy, and fueled by courage.

This kind of courage looks like this:

- Taking the First Leap
  - o Others say that the launch of a pilot program is too early.
  - o Making a hire others don't yet understand.
  - o Sunsetting is a legacy system that no longer serves the mission.
- Being Willing to Stand Alone, Temporarily
  - o Visionaries are not contrarians—but they are often lonely at first. They can hold tension while building trust.

- o They withstand silence, discomfort, and criticism because they understand leadership means going first.
- Choosing Action Over Perfection
  - o They know that momentum creates clarity. That some things can only be learned in motion.
  - o They launch with humility, review with rigor, and refine with care.
- Framing the Risk of Inaction
  - o They shift the narrative: "Here's what happens if we don't move."
  - o They help others see that waiting is sometimes the most dangerous decision.
- Creating Psychological Safety for Others to Follow
  - o By going first, they create permission. Their courage gives others room to take their first steps.
  - o They say, "You don't have to be certain— just committed. We'll build the path together."

True visionaries act before the applause. They take the unpopular stance, back it up with integrity, and invite others to test, learn, and evolve alongside them.

And over time, the very people who once hesitated began to follow—not because the risk has vanished, but because someone showed them what leading through belief looks like.

History doesn't remember the people who waited. It remembers those who moved first—and brought others with them.

Consensus can't be the prerequisite for action when the future is unclear. Vision has to lead. And courage has to follow.

Embedding Legacy into Daily Leadership

Legacy is not a retirement speech. It's not a plaque or a program that bears your name. Legacy is how people experience your leadership—today. And it's forged not in headlines but in the quiet, repeated choices you make when no one is watching.

Visionary leaders understand that legacy is not the destination. It's the trail you leave in real-time.

They know that every meeting, every decision, every reaction is a chance to encode values. It's not about being perfect—it's about being intentional.

Here's how legacy becomes a living force:

- Lead with Future Stakeholders in Mind
    - o Ask: "What will the next generation inherit from this decision?" That one question asked consistently, reshapes how priorities are set, conflicts are resolved, and value is defined.
    - o Think in terms of stewardship, not just strategy. What do you want your leadership to protect, grow, and evolve—long after you're gone?

- Make Decisions That Compound Over Time
  - o Invest in relationships, not just results. Build systems that others can improve, not just admire—design with future flexibility in mind.
  - o Legacy-minded leaders make trade-offs that look conservative today but create exponential resilience tomorrow.
- Codify What Matters
  - o Don't assume your values will outlive you—name them, teach them, and build them into the structures. Culture doesn't preserve itself. Leaders do.
  - o Whether it's how meetings begin, how hard news is delivered, or how ess is celebrated—legacy, legacy in the rituals you protect.
- Let Your Actions Teach
  - o Every time you handle conflict with empathy, choose long-term impact over short-term optics, or ask a better question—you're shaping what leadership means for those around you.
  - o You become the reference point. The example people silently cite when they say, "This is how we do things here."
- Institutionalize Reflection
  - o Encourage your teams to reflect not just on performance but on meaning. Build pause into pace. Make room for purpose.

- Create the Conditions for Continuity
  - o Don't just lead well—leave well. Develop succession strategies, mentor rising leaders, and design with a horizon longer than your tenure.
  - o The actual test of legacy is whether the system thrives after you're gone.
- Shape Culture Through Daily Behaviors
  - o From how you handle pressure to how you respond to setbacks, your responses build muscle memory in the organization.
  - o Leaders who model gratitude, curiosity, and humility create a culture that doesn't just perform—it endures.

Legacy is not about being remembered. It's about leaving behind a system that can keep moving forward with clarity, character, and compassion.

Visionary leaders make sure the future doesn't start after they leave. It starts now—in how they listen, decide, and serve.

"Legacy is not what follows your name. It's what others do more boldly because you led with intention."

— Sumit Sharma

Closing: The Final Turn

A book can end. But leadership doesn't.

The work of shaping healthcare's future is never finished—it is passed forward. Carried on the shoulders of those bold enough to imagine differently, act courageously, and care deeply.

If you are holding this book, you are already one of them. Not because of your title but because of your willingness to lead when it's hardest: when the data is incomplete, the path is unclear, and the stakes are profoundly human.

This book has not given you a script. It has offered a signal. This is a reminder that healthcare's next chapter won't be authored by policy alone, technology, or capital. It will be shaped by those brave enough to lead with vision, build with intention, and stay anchored in values when the winds of urgency blow strongest.

You are not managing complexity. You are designing coherence.

You are not reacting to the future. You are helping write it.

The visionary edge doesn't come from knowing all the answers. It comes from asking the questions that move us forward—together.

So, walk back into your work with a renewed sense of what's possible. Ask more. Listen deeper. Lead wider.

And when you feel like you're walking alone, remember:

"The future is not a forecast. It's a choice. And leadership is how we choose it."

— **Sumit Sharma**

Appendix: Tools + Frameworks for Visionary Healthcare Leadership

The VISION Framework

Purpose: A strategic leadership compass for navigating uncertainty.

Use Case: Helps leaders realign to purpose, reframe complexity, and act decisively in ambiguous times.

How to Use the VISION Framework

- **Strategic Retreats:** Use VISION to frame annual or quarterly offsite conversations. Ask your leadership team to reflect on how each letter shows up (or doesn't) in the current strategy.

- **Leadership Development:** Embed VISION into coaching, mentoring, and onboarding practices. Use it as a leadership self-assessment tool.
- **Crisis Navigation:** When faced with complex decisions, walk through the six principles. What does integrity look like here? How can optionality be preserved?
- **Narrative Design:** The "N" component designs town halls, vision statements, or transformation communications that inspire alignment.
- **Team Check-ins:** Rotate one letter per month in leadership meetings. Ask teams to discuss how they live that principle—and where they're stuck.

V - Values as Anchors

Return to core beliefs when decisions get murky. Ground yourself in what will never change, even when everything else shifts.

I - Inquiry Over Assumption

Curiosity is the antidote to rigidity. Ask better questions—challenge defaults. Let inquiry guide evolution.

S - Systems Thinking

See the whole, not just the part. Understand interdependencies, feedback loops, and how local changes affect global outcomes.

I - Integrity in Motion

Be consistent even when conditions aren't. Lead with alignment between intention, word, and action.

O - Optionality for Resilience

Design for flexibility. Don't build single-path plans. Keep options alive to respond to evolving futures.

N - Narrative as Strategy

The story is about how vision travels. Communicate where you're going, why it matters, and who belongs in the journey.

"VISION is not just a framework—it's a mindset. One that sees uncertainty as an invitation to lead."

— **Sumit Sharma**

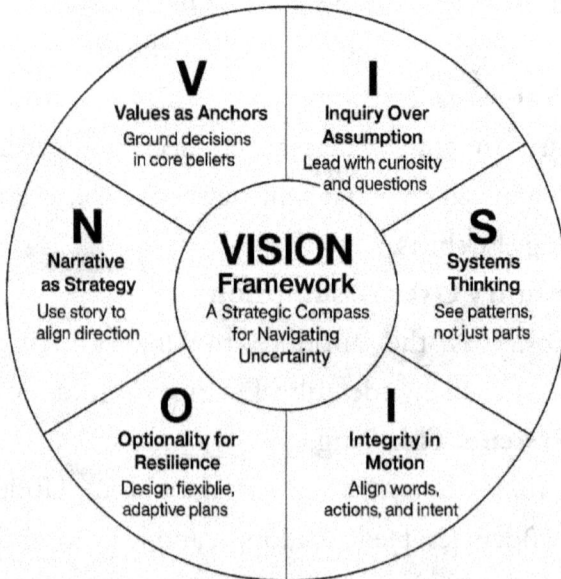

VISION Framework — A Strategic Compass for Navigating Uncertainty

- **V** — Values as Anchors: Ground decisions in core beliefs
- **I** — Inquiry Over Assumption: Lead with curiosity and questions
- **S** — Systems Thinking: See patterns, not just parts
- **I** — Integrity in Motion: Align words, actions, and intent
- **O** — Optionality for Resilience: Design flexible, adaptive plans
- **N** — Narrative as Strategy: Use story to align direction

The Strategic Elasticity Grid

Purpose: A diagnostic tool to evaluate how well a healthcare system can flex under pressure, adapt to change, and scale transformation without losing integrity.

Use Case: Use this framework in strategic planning sessions, board discussions, or operational reviews to assess where your system is rigid, adaptive, or resilient across core enterprise dimensions.

STRATEGIC ELASTICITY GRID

Domains of Operation	Fixed Rigid, legacy-bound	Flexible Adaptable within defined boundaries	Fluid Continuously evolving, dynamic
Clinical Delivery	Fixed care pathways	Some modular models	Fully adaptive, team-based care
Digital Infrastructure	Siloed legacy IT	API integration	Cloud-native, predictive systems
Operatioinal Efficiency	Manual workflows	Process automation	AI-driven orchestration
Workforce Strategy	Rigid org charts	Cross-training encouraged	Role-fluidity + internal redeployment
Governance & Leadership	Top-down committees	Agile steering groups	Distributed, network-based leadership

The Grid Dimensions

Axes:

Horizontal Axis (Domains of Operation):

- Clinical Delivery
- Digital Infrastructure
- Operational Efficiency
- Workforce Strategy
- Governance & Leadership

Vertical Axis (Levels of Elasticity):

- Fixed – Rigid, inflexible, often legacy-bound
- Flexible – Adaptable within defined boundaries
- Fluid – Dynamic, responsive, continuously evolving

Example Grid Application:

Domain	Fixed	Flexible	Fluid
Clinical Delivery	Fixed care pathways only	Some modular clinical models	Fully team-based, adaptive care models
Digital Infrastructure	Siloed legacy IT systems	Some integration with APIs	Cloud-native, predictive platforms
Operational Efficiency	Manual workflows	Select process automation	AI-driven orchestration
Workforce Strategy	Fixed roles, rigid org chart	Cross-training encouraged	Team fluidity, talent redeployment
Governance	Top-down, slow committees	Agile steering groups	Distributed, data-driven decision rights

How to Use the Strategic Elasticity Grid:

1. Assess: Rate each domain across the three elasticity levels with your leadership team.
2. Discuss: Identify areas of rigidity that create drag and places of high fluidity that could be scaled.
3. Design: Use insights to create an elasticity roadmap—outlining what to preserve, evolve, or let go.
4. Track: Revisit annually to track transformation maturity.

"Elastic systems don't just absorb shock—they grow stronger through disruption."

— Sumit Sharma

The Culture-as-OS Canvas

Purpose: Diagnose how your organizational culture functions as the operating system behind every action, decision, and transformation effort.

Use Case: Use during leadership retreats, transformation planning, or culture reset moments to understand how your cultural architecture is either accelerating or obstructing change.

Inputs:

- Core Assumptions: What do people believe is rewarded, punished, or ignored?

- Rituals & Routines: What is repeated and normalized? How are meetings conducted?
- Power Signals: Who speaks, decides, and challenges your system?
- Feedback Loops: How does truth surface and act upon?
- Psychological Safety: Do people feel safe to share dissent or failure?
- How to Use:
- Map your organization using the five inputs.
- Discuss whether these patterns serve or block your mission.
- Identify one cultural behavior to shift in each category.
- Implement with visible leadership modeling.
- Reassess quarterly to ensure intentional culture-building.

"Culture is not a backdrop—it's the invisible code that runs every visible result."

— Sumit Sharma

The Signal Scanning Radar

Purpose: Create a repeatable process to identify early change signals across healthcare domains.

Use Case: For strategic foresight, innovation planning, and scenario development.

SIGNAL SCANNING RADAR

A FORESIGHT TOOL FOR HEALTHCARE LEADERS

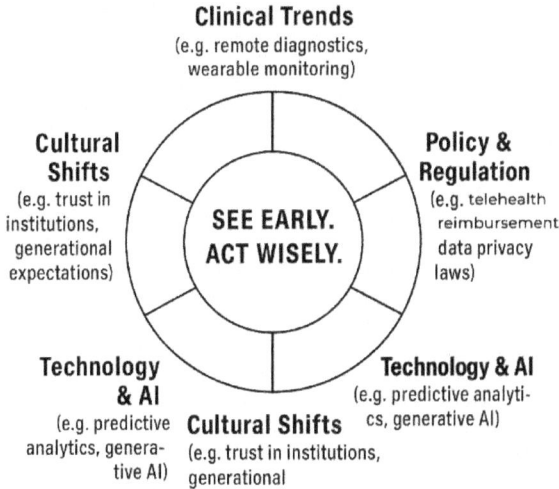

Clinical Trends
(e.g. remote diagnostics, wearable monitoring)

Cultural Shifts
(e.g. trust in institutions, generational expectations)

SEE EARLY. ACT WISELY.

Policy & Regulation
(e.g. telehealth reimbursement data privacy laws)

Technology & AI
(e.g. predictive analytics, generative AI)

Technology & AI
(e.g. predictive analytics, generative AI)

Cultural Shifts
(e.g. trust in institutions, generational

How to Use
1. Assign teams to each domain
2. Scan monthly or quarterly for weak signals
3. Identify early indicators worth exploring further
4. Integrate findings into strategy

"Leaders don't just react to trends—they develop the muscle to see what's coming before it arrives."

— Sumit Sharma

The Legacy Loop

Purpose: Embed long-term thinking into short-term decision-making to ensure that every action contributes to a sustainable and value-aligned future.

Use Case: Executive decision-making, succession planning, and leadership development.

The Five Stages of the Legacy Loop:

- Intention: Start every initiative by asking: What legacy are we trying to build?
- Impact: Consider the near-term and downstream effects of the action.
- Inheritance: Who will receive the outcome of this decision? Are they equipped?
- Iteration: What feedback do we need to learn and adjust?
- Intention (Revisited): Has our purpose changed, and if so, how does that reshape our next step?

How to Use:

- Apply to major strategic decisions (e.g., facility expansions, tech investments, cultural redesigns).
- It can be used as a coaching tool with leaders to review decisions using the loop.
- Build into board or executive templates (e.g., "Legacy Impact" slide).
- Revisit annually in succession and vision planning.

The Legacy Loop

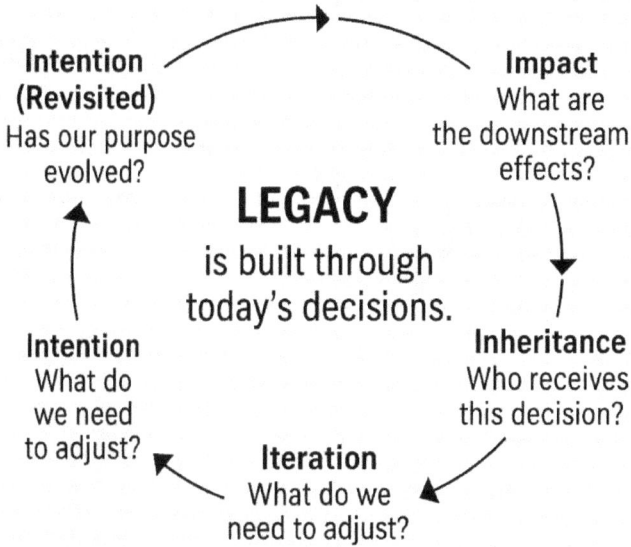

Intention (Revisited)
Has our purpose evolved?

Impact
What are the downstream effects?

LEGACY
is built through today's decisions.

Inheritance
Who receives this decision?

Intention
What do we need to adjust?

Iteration
What do we need to adjust?

"Legacy isn't built at the finish line—it's forged in every daily decision made with future eyes."

— Sumit Sharma

Interested in a Future in Healthcare Leadership?

If you're passionate about leadership and curious about careers in healthcare, you may enjoy my other book, Transforming the Operating Room: Innovative Leadership Strategies for Surgical Efficiency. This book dives into the real-world challenges and leadership skills needed to improve surgical teams and hospital efficiency. Whether you aspire to be a doctor, nurse, administrator, or healthcare innovator, understanding healthcare leadership will give you a head start. Here is the link https://a.co/d/0HAaoFy

www.ingramcontent.com/pod-product-compliance
Lightning Source LLC
Chambersburg PA
CBHW052120270326
41930CB00012B/2698